TOP
BIRDING SITES
of Europe

TOP
BIRDING SITES
of Europe

DOMINIC COUZENS

First published in 2011 by New Holland Publishers

London • Cape Town • Sydney • Auckland

www.newhollandpublishers.com

Garfield House, 86-88 Edgware Road, London W2 2EA, United Kingdom

80 McKenzie Street, Cape Town, 8001, South Africa

Unit 1, 66 Gibbes Street, Chatswood, NSW 2067, Australia

218 Lake Road, Northcote, Auckland, New Zealand

10 9 8 7 6 5 4 3 2 1

A CIP catalogue record for this book is available from the British Library.

ISBN 978 1 84773 767 0

Publisher: Simon Papps

Editor: Elaine Rose

Photography: AGAMI (photographers listed on page 190)

Designer: Nicola Liddiard

Production: Melanie Dowland

Reproduction by Pica Digital PTE Ltd, Singapore

Printed and bound in Singapore by Tien Wah Press (PTE) Ltd

Front cover: Bar-tailed Godwits

Back cover: Northern Hawk Owl

Page 1: Great Northern Diver

Page 3: Atlantic Puffin

Opposite: Tengmalm's Owl

Pages 6-7: Mixed wader flock

Page 8: Juvenile Black-crowned Night Heron (above) and European Roller (below)

Page 9: White-tailed Eagle

Contents

This book is a celebration of the birds of Europe. Through the description of 30 of the continent's top birding sites, it gives an overall view of the variety and abundance of avian delights that can be enjoyed in our corner of the world. It isn't a site guide, giving you detailed directions as to where to go in order to see a certain species: there are plenty of these on the market already. Instead it is a book to get you inspired, suggesting broadly where the best places are to have great experiences watching European birds in their natural habitat.

The concept for this book came from *Top 100 Birding Sites of the World*, published in 2008, which gave a worldwide spread. Seventeen of the sites in that book came from Europe, and all of them are included here, with updates and amendments. Each site has its own section, with a description of the place, the habitat it encompasses, what birds occur there and, overall, why it is included in the book. Hopefully, the uniqueness of the place will come across and the descriptions of what is found there will go well beyond a banal list of what has been recorded.

The obvious question any reader will ask is: how were the sites chosen? What right did each have to be included? The title *Top Birding Sites of Europe* suggests that there is a hierarchy among birding sites and that some are better than others. And while this is undoubtedly true, the reasons behind any site's inclusion in this book have been necessarily complex and not always empirical. For example, I have attempted to include a good geographical spread, which means that, where two sites have similar merit, one will be chosen over another if it is in a part of

Europe without another entry in the book. Secondly, I have also been careful to allow for a good spread of habitats, so there are mountains, grasslands and forests as well as species-rich deltas and migration hot spots.

At this point, it should be mentioned that the book has kept fairly strict boundaries as to what is Europe. These days birders tend to think in terms of the 'Western Palearctic' rather than Europe, encompassing, as it does, the very similar and easily appreciated birds of North Africa and the Middle East. However, the problem here is that there are so many great sites in these outlying regions that the book would have had to include 50 instead of 30 places if there was any meaningful representation in the heart of Western Europe. So, regrettably, I have had to exclude such marvellous places as Turkey, the Canary Islands and the Caucasus.

Apart from the considerations given above, here is a list of the other factors that went into the choice of sites: the sheer quality of birds to be found there (how rare, how beautiful, in spectacular numbers, etc); how important the site is on a world scale for the conservation of the relevant habitat and/or species; the intrinsic beauty of the site; the degree to which a site is good all year; the history and both ornithological and environmental significance of the site; the ease and comfort of birding the site, where relevant; the possibility of delighting in other features, such as other animals or natural or archaeological spectaculars; and yes, perhaps, the fame and star quality of the place, too.

In the end, despite all this, the selection of sites was, of necessity and expedience, a matter of my own experience, and I expect to stir up some arguments and emotions by presenting this finished product to you. You will doubtless be appalled that certain of your favourites are excluded and you will be even more aggravated by what is included instead. That is part of the joy, and the peril, of publishing such a book. Furthermore, for a bit of fun and deliberate provocation, I have also included a ranking of the sites from 1 to 30. Please feel free to write infuriated communications in response.

It is important to state, in closing, that all the selections were made free from commercial pressure. None will have known for sure that they have been included in this book before publication and no one paid for the privilege. Nobody offered or gave free accommodation during the research, either.

I do hope that this book will succeed in its ultimate aim: to enthuse you to bask in the riches of Europe's birdlife.

Dominic Couzens, Dorset, UK

Spring 2011

ACKNOWLEDGEMENTS

Thanks, as ever, to Simon Papps, my patient publisher at New Holland, and to editor Elaine Rose for poring over the many details included in this book. And a big thank you Nicola Liddiard for making such a good job of designing the cover and spreads.

DEDICATION

To the team at home: wife Carolyn and children Emily and Samuel. Here's hoping we can explore some of these sites together.

10 The Azores

INFORMATION

SITE RANK | 17

HABITAT | Volcanic islands with crater lakes, cultivation, some native laurel woodland. Occasional small wetlands, coasts, harbours

KEY SPECIES | Azores Bullfinch, Island Canary, Cory's Shearwater, rare seabirds, vagrants

TIME OF YEAR | Best time is from early summer through to November

Very much a western outpost of Europe, the Azores archipelago lies some 1,500km from the coast of Portugal, in mid-Atlantic Ocean, and 3,900km from the coast of North America. In such a state of isolation, it has a limited avifauna of breeding birds and, until recently, was largely disregarded by birdwatchers. But after several recent discoveries, coupled with curiosity about the islands' critically endangered bullfinch, the Azores are now very much on the ornithological map and provide a niche market for adventurous, pioneering visitors.

The archipelago is composed of nine main islands, which are spread out over 600km of ocean from west to east. For convenience, the islands are divided into three groups: the eastern group of São Miguel and Santa Maria; the central group of Terceira, Pico, Graciosa, São Jorge and Faial; and the western group, which includes the small outlying islands of Flores and Corvo. It is a vast area but quite ornithologically homogeneous. As a general rule, most of the land birds are found on most of the islands but sometimes the same species are represented by different races. For example, the Goldcrest has one subspecies on São Miguel, another on Santa Maria and yet another on the rest of the islands.

The basic land avifauna is a weird concoction of familiar forms from Europe, with many gaps left by birds that have never made it here. Widespread and common species are Blackcap, European Robin, Common Blackbird, Common Starling, House Sparrow, Goldfinch, Chaffinch, Common Buzzard, Feral Pigeon and

Common Woodpigeon, while many very abundant continental species, such as Common Whitethroat, White Wagtail, Tree Sparrow, Common Cuckoo and Barn Swallow, are missing. There are a few much scarcer breeding species too, including Common Quail, Red-legged Partridge, Common Moorhen, Kentish Plover, Eurasian Woodcock, Common Snipe, Long-eared Owl and two recent arrivals, the Collared Dove and Common Waxbill. One of the more unexpected settlers has been the Grey Wagtail, of all things, which is common on every island. Following the rule that in the absence of competition a species can expand its niche, the Grey Wagtail is found not only on streams and rivers here but also on woodland edge, in farmland, beaches and settlements.

One clear influence of the Macaronesian avifauna (that of the Atlantic islands, including the Canaries and Madeira) is the presence of the Island Canary, which is common. This small finch, closely related to the Serin, occurs from sea level to the volcanic mountain tops, in both cultivated and natural habitats. It has certainly adapted better to change than its relative, the endangered Azores Bullfinch (there are no bullfinches on the Canaries or Madeira). This species, larger than its continental counterpart and with male and female looking alike, is now confined

Opposite: The Azores has a temperate, lush climate, with mild winters, warm summers and plenty of rain.

Above: The Azores Bullfinch is slightly larger than its continental counterpart and the sexes are alike, with the male lacking any bright pink on the underparts. It is confined to native laurel forest on São Miguel.

to the island of São Miguel and just in a single locality, the Pico da Vara, where there is enough growth of the original natural laurel forest for it to survive. Within this 102km² range there are 1,608 ± 326 mature individuals. For a few months of the year this species is entirely dependent on a small number of native trees and this is its Achilles heel. Only serious conservation efforts are keeping it alive.

Not surprisingly, since the Azores are in mid-Atlantic Ocean, the seabirds here are a great deal more impressive in both number and variety than the common land birds. Nobody could possibly escape seeing the hordes of Cory's Shearwaters, for instance, which are everywhere around the coasts. Up to 188,000 pairs breed, well over 10 per cent of the world population. In the summer their cacophanous, demented wailing calls echo from the cliffs and craggy areas, often well inland, while at sea it is almost impossible to view any stretch of ocean hereabouts without one of these lazy-flying shearwaters passing your field of view.

Other common and easily seen breeding species include the local race of the Yellow-legged Gull, sometimes called the Atlantic or even Azorean Gull, which could one day be in line for separation from other Yellow-legged Gulls, with its much darker flecking on the head in winter. About 2,800 pairs breed on the

Below: One of the seabird specialities of the Azores, the Bulwer's Petrel maintains a small, scattered population of 50 pairs.

Opposite: There have been nearly 30 records of the vagrant Great Blue Heron up to June 2010, more than in the rest of the Western Palearctic combined.

Opposite above: A Wood Duck on the Azores is far more likely to be of wild origin than a bird recorded in continental Europe.

Opposite below: The stunning Northern Parula is one of an incredible 16 species of New World Warblers to have been seen in the Azores up to the middle of 2010. Both records have been on Corvo.

CD tracks

TRACK 1: Cory's Shearwater
TRACK 2: Blackcap

archipelago, on every island. Meanwhile, there are perhaps 4,000 pairs of Common Tern and 1,000 pairs of Roseate Tern, the latter comprising over half the European population of this fast-declining species. Meanwhile, there are some 115 pairs of Manx Shearwater, mainly on Corvo and Flores.

It is, though, the less familiar breeding and visiting seabirds that make the Azores particularly interesting to the European birder. For example, there is a small population of Macaronesian Shearwater, amounting to about 150 pairs, on Ilhéu de Vila, off Santa Maria, and two islets off Graciosa – Praia and Baixo – and an even smaller, scattered population of some 50 pairs of Bulwer's Petrel in scattered sites, including Ilhéu de Vila again. Meanwhile, the Madeiran Storm-petrel is more numerous, with 800 breeding pairs. These birds are unique among European birds (and almost unique in the world) in having two separate breeding seasons, with different birds using the same breeding burrows – a sort of shift system. 'Hot season' birds begin breeding in May, while 'cool season' birds start off in September. There are 200 hot season pairs on Ilhéu de Praia and Baixo and 400 cold season pairs. Despite being ever present, these birds only visit their burrows at night and are difficult to see at sea. The two shifts may represent different species; at least some have dubbed the summer-breeding birds as 'Monteiro's Storm-petrels'.

But what else breeds on the Azores? Certainly the Sooty Tern has recently begun breeding in minute numbers on the islets mentioned above, with the downy chick recorded in 1994 constituting the first breeding record for Europe. The previous year, in September 1993, an adult Red-billed Tropicbird was recorded incubating an egg on Ilhéu de Baixo, marking a similar first for that species. What about other seabirds, such as the Fea's Petrel, recently trapped in the breeding season? There is much yet to discover about the seabirds of this area.

In fact, Sooty Terns and Red-billed Tropicbirds are not the only breeding oddities to have occurred in the Azores. Others include, of all things, the American Black Duck. In the past there have been so many of these on the islands that they have actually met up and reproduced. This phenomenon, at first seemingly freakish, is actually a symptom of a broader trend: the sheer numbers of American birds on the Azores archipelago. Despite the long distance, there are always some American birds here, and it is far and away the best place in Europe to see them.

Some are positively numerous: Ring-necked Duck and Blue-winged Teal are annual, while White-rumped Sandpiper is commoner than Dunlin or Little Stint. American gulls are numerous. The celebrated Cabo de Praia on Terceira, a very small and insignificant-looking flooded quarry, has hosted no less than 17 species of Nearctic waders, often four or five at the same time. The various lakes and ponds regularly host American Coot, Pied-billed Grebe and Great Blue Heron.

Double-crested Cormorant records greatly outnumber those of Great Cormorant and there have been more records of Belted Kingfisher than Common Kingfisher.

Nowhere is the trend of American birds more pronounced than on the two westernmost islands, Corvo and Flores, in the late autumn. Starting in earnest in 2005, pioneers have begun to cover these islands at the right times and have made some incredible discoveries. Every year since, they have uncovered new birds for the Azores and sometimes for the entire Western Palearctic – White-eyed Vireo, for instance, in 2005. Some of these have come in groups, such as Chimney Swift (27 on Corvo in 2005), Indigo Bunting (6 on Corvo the same year), Bobolink (2 on Flores in 2008) and Dickcissel (2 on Flores in 2009). No year has passed without a clutch of American land birds, such as warblers, vireos and chats, together with a sprinkling of unlikely species such as Paddyfield Warbler (2008) and Citrine Wagtail (2009), and there is no doubt that the trend will now continue. These islands, together with the Azores as a whole, are now in the forefront of rarity finding in Europe. It's a new frontier.

16

Straits of Gibraltar

INFORMATION

SITE RANK | 10

HABITAT | Sea coast, low hills, cultivation, rocky outcrops

KEY SPECIES | Migrating raptors and seabirds, Barbary Partridge, some passerines

TIME OF YEAR | Interesting all year but the peak migration times are July to October and March to May

You only need to look at a map of Europe to suspect that the Straits of Gibraltar might be interesting for birds. Since vast numbers of migrants travel between Europe and Africa every year, one might suspect, instinctively, that the narrowest point between the two continents could be the scene of a significant migratory phenomenon. And for once, the intuitive conclusion is absolutely correct. Gibraltar and the nearby Spanish coast constitute one of the busiest migration bottlenecks in the world, with hundreds of thousands of birds passing every year, especially in the autumn. Those species to whom a narrow crossing and a short journey are more important than most, such as birds of prey and storks, gather here in their thousands.

A stretch of coastline about 40km long between Tarifa in the west and the Rock of Gibraltar in the east is covered by this section. Much of it consists of unremarkable beaches, rocky coast and rolling hills, together with various villages and towns with their attendant gardens and cultivation. The Rock of Gibraltar itself, though, is an unmistakable feature of the landscape, a curious promontory made up from a huge limestone rock 426m high, which towers over its neighbouring landscape and doesn't quite seem to fit. The Rock plays host to a tiny, overcrowded independent country affiliated to the UK, separate from Spain and 25km from the nearby coast of North Africa.

Although the Rock of Gibraltar is the best-known site for observing the flights of large birds and usually offers the closest views of them, as they sometimes seem to skim the top of the Rock, the nearby Spanish coast can prove equally attractive, especially around the small settlement of Tarifa, where the straits are only 14km wide. Different wind conditions influence which birds are most numerous where, with Gibraltar itself being favoured during westerly winds and Tarifa when the wind is easterly. Counts are made every year along the stretch from Punta del Carnero, near Algeciras, to Facinas, 20km north-west of Tarifa, so that the flight as a whole is accurately recorded.

And what a flight it is! In autumn, over 250,000 birds of prey may pass over on their way south, with much smaller numbers (15,000–20,000) moving north in the spring; there are also about 50,000 White Storks and 1,000 Black Storks annually. About 25 species of raptor have been recorded and some of these move in impressive numbers. European Honey-buzzards are the dominant species, with 70,000–100,000 passing, but other regular counts include 75,000 Black Kites, 5,000 Griffon Vultures, 5,000 Short-toed Eagles, 2,700–5,000 Eurasian

Opposite: At their narrowest point, the Straits of Gibraltar are only 14km wide, separating the continents of Europe and Africa.

Sparrowhawks, 5,000 Booted Eagles and up to 2,000 Montagu's Harriers. Not surprisingly, these figures are spiced up with plenty of variety, including regular Black Vulture, Red Kite, Northern Goshawk, Bonelli's and Spanish Imperial Eagles, Lesser Kestrel, Lanner Falcon and, somewhat surprisingly, eastern specialities such as Lesser and Greater Spotted Eagles. It is certainly a good place to hone those bird of prey identification skills.

One unexpected recent trend has been the growing number of records of what was hitherto considered an exclusively African species, the Rüppell's Vulture. This species was first recorded in Iberia in 1992 and since then has become an annual visitor, sometimes in numbers (there were six together at Tarifa in 2005). It is thought that their recent appearance in Spain can be attributed to the changing behaviour of the closely related Griffon Vulture, which is wintering in greater numbers in sub-Saharan Africa. As the Griffons migrate north in spring, they bring the Rüppell's Vultures along with them, especially the juveniles. The latter species, therefore, may have a reasonable chance of colonizing Spain in the coming years.

Each species that passes through the Straits of Gibraltar has its own particular flight time, which means that interest in the area can be maintained pretty much for ten months of the year (February to November). February at the Rock of Gibraltar brings the first trickle of early species, such as Common and Lesser Kestrels, Egyptian Vulture, Black Kite, Western Marsh Harrier and Osprey. All these species increase in number in March, which is their peak spring month, as it is also for Short-toed Eagle. A good day in March can produce 10–15 species of raptor but April has more consistent variety. For its part, April is the best month for Red Kite and Booted Eagle, while the main streams of European Honey-buzzard don't pass until May. They are late migrants because of their need to feed on wasp grubs, which aren't around until the late spring. The Hobby, too, is a late migrant, which will be feeding its young on the midsummer production of fledgling birds in Europe's open country.

Fun though the spring is, it is the autumn that really gets the birders' juices flowing. Again, there is the tempting trickle of Black Kites and Lesser Kestrels to set things off in July, with large numbers of the former passing in August and finishing their migration early. In September, with favourable winds, the very best flights occur, with up to 10,000 raptors per day. European Honey-buzzards appear in a short burst in early September, while other species that peak this month include Booted and Short-toed Eagles and Egyptian Vulture. October and November, while less spectacular, are good for harriers, Common Buzzard and sometimes Griffon Vultures.

Opposite: European Honey-buzzards are the most numerous raptors passing over the Straits. They peak in early September, when thousands may pass in a single day.

Above: White-rumped Swift is one of the European rarities that breeds just inland from the Straits of Gibraltar.

Above: Migrating Black Kites are numerous at the Straits. They tend to kick the migration seasons off, appearing in February and again as early as July.

CD tracks

TRACK 3: Black Kite
TRACK 4: Yellow-legged Gull

Impressive though these figures are, this does not guarantee that a visit will instantly ensure that hundreds of shapes can be seen flying past, even in season. In common with the situation at other hawk-watches, weather conditions determine events, with a flight of thousands one day being followed by disappointment the next. In autumn, poor weather will see an accumulation of storks and other birds in the general area as the migrants wait for their chance to cross. Once the weather clears, thousands of birds will set off all at once and the flight will be over in a day or two. It is essential for most birds, especially the broader-winged birds that usually rely on thermals, to cross when it is safe to do so. Too much easterly wind could blow them out to the Atlantic, whilst strong winds and rain could ditch them into the straits.

If there isn't much going on in the sky, a birder's attention could be drawn instead to the waters of the straits themselves. They can, in fact, be superb for seawatching and would perhaps be more famous as such were it not for the regular spectaculars in the sky. Scarce species such as Audouin's Gull, Balearic and

Yelkouan Shearwaters and Lesser Crested Tern are regular, especially from Europa Point in Gibraltar and Playa de los Lances (Tarifa), while watches in spring and autumn will routinely reveal such birds as Black Scoter, Northern Gannet, Arctic and Great Skuas, Black, Common and Sandwich Terns and the ubiquitous Yellow-legged Gull. Every year brings rarities and these have included Macaronesian Shearwater, Royal Tern and Laughing Gull. While most birders come during passage period, the sea here can be excellent at any time of year.

There isn't much space here to talk about passerine migration or breeding birds but there are highlights among these too. Cold fronts often bring small falls of migratory passerines to the Rock of Gibraltar, involving warblers and chats of a variety of species, and over the years a long and impressive list of these has been accumulated. Meanwhile, there are several unusual breeding birds in the area. The Rock of Gibraltar hosts the only population of Barbary Partridge on the mainland of Europe, which delight many birders, despite having almost certainly been introduced by man many years ago. Inland, there are rarities including White-rumped and Little Swifts and Black-winged Kite. All this ensures that, even on the quiet days for migration, the birder visiting here will never be bored.

Below: The Rock of Gibraltar holds mainland Europe's only breeding Barbary Partridges, although they were probably introduced deliberately from North Africa.

22 Coto Doñana

SITE RANK | 2

HABITAT | Seasonally flooded marshes (*marismas*), salt flats, woodland, scrub, dunes, beach

KEY SPECIES | Herons and egrets, Red-knobbed Coot, Marbled and Ferruginous Ducks, Purple Swamp-hen, Spanish Imperial Eagle

TIME OF YEAR | All year, although July and August are poor for waterbirds

Opposite: The enormous wetlands of the Coto Doñana are, unsurprisingly, ideal for herons such as this Black-crowned Night Heron.

It seems almost unbelievable that there could be a 1,300km² tract of unspoilt wilderness left anywhere in Western Europe. But, give or take a small amount of development, that's what you get in the Coto de Doñana National Park, in southern Spain. Here, at the mouth of the Rio Guadalquivir, you can lose yourself in huge expanses of marshland, dune, beach and pine wood, and begin to imagine what the primeval state of this part of southern Europe must once have looked like. It is a humbling experience.

Not surprisingly, given the abuse suffered by most of Spain's southern coastline, it is something of a freak of history that Doñana, as it is universally known, has survived reasonably intact to the present day. Indeed, the seeds for its preservation date back to the 1600s, when the area was in the hands of the Dukes of Medina Sidonia. These owners appreciated its excellence as a good hunting area (it had enjoyed such a reputation since at least 1200), kept it relatively pristine and, crucially, made a habit of inviting royalty to visit. The kings' stopovers became great events (King Felipe IV was reputed to have brought an entourage of 12,000 people in spring 1624) and thus, for 300 years or so, the incumbent monarchs would descend from time to time upon Doñana, shoot a few head of game and compliment the current duke upon his fine estate. With the seal of royal approval, the area remained safe in the hands of generations of complimented dukes and escaped the bulldozed fate of much of the rest of southern Spain.

Even in 1953, this was still a remote area. In that year a team of naturalists, led by the late distinguished British ornithologist and conservationist Guy Mountfort, visited Doñana and carried out scientific research, including counts and descriptions of the birdlife. The resulting account of this and subsequent expeditions, *Portrait of a Wilderness*, with its evocative descriptions of a lost world not so far away from enraptured readers, where the sun shone and the only mode of transport was on horseback, became something of a bestseller. This entrenched the Coto Doñana's reputation as one of the most exciting places in Europe for birdwatching and gave it something of an aura. Happily, and emphatically, in the 50 years since, it has maintained its reputation and is almost as good as it ever was.

The Coto Doñana is what you might call a failed delta. In sluggish old age, many a river breaks into dozens of small channels as it lurches towards the sea. However, owing to the action of ocean and wind, all but one of the Guadalquivir's routes to the sea have been blocked by a large system of sand dunes that, over the

Above: One of the jewels in Doñana's crown is the stable population of the endangered Spanish Imperial Eagle: there are about seven pairs. The pale head, body and wing coverts identify this bird as a juvenile.

centuries, has built up on the coastal side. Thus, these days, there is but one river mouth, and a vast area of flat land hemmed in by the dunes is seasonally flooded by winter rains, usually to not much more than 1m in depth. The resulting marshlands are known as *marismas* and provide an enormous area of bird habitat. Together with the dunes, salt flats and patches of Mediterranean-type scrub formed by various aromatic plants, and with woodland on the higher ground, these marshlands provide a patchwork of rich habitats, attracting an astonishing variety of birds. Up to 2010, 380 species have been recorded, of which a staggering 150 regularly breed.

With so much shallow water about, it is hardly surprising that the heron family does very well here. Several species maintain populations in the hundreds of pairs, including the Purple Heron (minimum 300 pairs), Little and Cattle Egrets and Black-crowned Night Heron. Squacco Heron and Little Bittern are present in lower numbers but can be easier to see here than in many other parts of Europe. Most of these species breed in mixed colonies, often in the cork oaks in the woodlands, but Purple Heron and Little Bittern are solitary breeders. In recent years the Great White Egret, once so mysteriously rare in Europe as a whole, has become a familiar sight in the area.

The herons don't hold the monopoly on long-legged wading birds in Doñana. An increasing population (now 1,000 pairs) of Glossy Ibis is present, along with about 400 pairs of Eurasian Spoonbill, often mixed in with the breeding colonies of herons, while there are always some non-breeding Greater Flamingos about in the shallow, saline waters. White Storks are abundant, and the largest colony in Europe, 400 pairs, is found in the north of the reserve. Meanwhile, both Black-winged Stilt and Pied Avocet are a familiar sight on the salt pans or saline pools, with thousands of pairs breeding. It might be stretching the point to call the Purple Swamp-hen long-legged, but these 'big-nosed', iridescent blue lumps are increasingly common in Doñana, despite being rare and localized in Europe overall.

Several other great rarities for Europe occur in Doñana. One of these, the Red-knobbed Coot, is mainly a bird of sub-Saharan Africa but occurs here in a relict population shared with the Maghreb. Once, finding this species required a patient

Below: The Ferruginous Duck, rare this far west in Europe, occasionally breeds. Note the broad white wing-bar.

check through thousands of Eurasian Coots, but researchers are now putting collars on individuals to make them easier to study and conserve. The secretive Marbled Duck, not found in Europe outside Spain and remarkable for its sheer sluggishness, still occurs in very small numbers. However, time has probably already run out for the Small Buttonquail, which is also known by its old name of Andalusian Hemipode. Unless the park authorities are keeping information quiet, the last Doñana record of this species was in 1999, so it is now probably extinct here. The Spanish Imperial Eagle is faring somewhat better, with a stable population of about seven pairs. In recent years, a shortage of rabbits has made life difficult for these specialists, but measures are being put in place to increase the population of the eagle's favourite food and its future seems reasonably secure.

If you visit Doñana in the winter you may notice – if you are not distracted by the 60,000 Greylag Geese, 100,000 Eurasian Teal and host of other wildfowl – that quite a few familiar faces remain behind when they should, by all accounts, be deep into Africa. The most obvious is probably the Barn Swallow, but other migrants, such as White Stork, Black Kite, Lesser Kestrel, Whiskered Tern and Common House Martin, regularly stay put and could all be considered resident. Clearly, impending climate change could soon add to this list, with birds altering their migratory journeys as the need for transcontinental movement is removed.

Below: The Red-knobbed Coot's European range is confined to a handful of sites in southern Spain. It can be hard to find among the thousands of Common Coots here.

Above: A winter's day dawns on the *Marismas*.

Doñana also attracts some astonishing rarities from Africa, and the trickle of these could perhaps turn into a more substantial feature in years to come. Among the more interesting are Pink-backed Pelican, African Spoonbill, Yellow-billed Stork and Marabou, while the Lesser Flamingo, recorded here several times recently, actually bred in Spain in the summer of 2007, although not here. Who knows what might colonize next.

The fabulous Coto Doñana has been one of Europe's top wetland sites for a great many years and excites continuing affection and delight among birders throughout Europe. It is thus scandalous that, on the whole, the Spanish government, which owns most of the land, has generally treated Doñana with contemptible disregard. One might think that it would recognize the site as the jewel it is and yet Doñana faces constant threats from development and other forms of abuse. In 1998 a chemical spill upstream nearly reached Doñana and would have done but for some last-minute building of dykes that only just averted wide-scale disastrous damage. The needs of tourism and development around the site lower the water table and chemicals leach into the Guadalquivir from nearby agri-business. The attitude of the Spanish government threatens not just the wildlife but a special part of Spanish history, too.

CD tracks

TRACK 5: Greylag Goose
TRACK 6: White Stork

Extremadura

INFORMATION

SITE RANK | 9

HABITAT | Steppe, rolling farmland, open woodland, scrub, rugged mountainsides, small towns

KEY SPECIES | Great and Little Bustards, Pin-tailed and Black-bellied Sandgrouse, Black Vulture, Spanish Imperial Eagle, Iberian Azure-winged Magpie

TIME OF YEAR | All year, although April to June is best for the breeding birds

It could be argued that Extremadura is the ornithological heart of Spain. True, the average visitor will log more species on a few days in the Coto Doñana, the Ebro Delta, or even along the southern coast. But when it comes to mega-populations of what we might think of as quintessentially Iberian birds, this quiet and peaceful region some 250km south-west of Madrid is like a vast, benign bank, where the loose change that you see is secured by vast riches stored away out of sight in the bountiful landscape. There are estimated to be, for example, a million pairs of Spotless Starling, 250,000 pairs of Woodchat Shrike, 100,000 pairs of Melodious Warbler and 200,000 pairs of Eurasian Hoopoe in Extremadura, to name but four species that are the everyday currency of birding in this part of the world.

Made up from two provinces, Badajoz and Cáceres, both of which are bordered by Portugal to the west, this is a sparsely populated, peaceful area of the Spanish hinterland, with rolling hills, scattered farmsteads, Mediterranean-type scrub, rich deciduous woodland, reservoirs and steppe-like grassland, its wide vistas and undisturbed landscapes in many ways presenting a throwback to a time when most people worked the land and high-intensity agriculture had not yet entered the vocabulary. Some parts, indeed, have hardly charged since medieval times. It is a refreshing place to visit and an inspiring region indeed to look for birds.

In terms of ornithology and conservation, Extremadura's most important habitat is its steppe, which is dotted about the region, with major patches close to Merida, Cáceres and Trujillo. This rolling grassland holds one of the most significant populations of Great and Little Bustards in the world, never mind Europe. About 17,000 pairs of Little Bustard occur and, until recently, were known to gather in flocks of more than 1,000 individuals, while Great Bustards still number 6,500 birds (counted 2008). So Extremadura ranks as one of the easiest places in the world to see these shy terrestrial birds. All you need to do is to stop on one of the many minor roads and scan likely areas. Displaying Great Bustards, which seem to ruffle up their plumage into a lather, often resemble sheep from a distance, so don't fall into the trap of wondering where all these sought-after birds are among the livestock. Large males hold court and dominate copulations with the local females. Male Little Bustards, meanwhile, sometimes combine several displays at once, stamping their feet, leaping into the air while flashing white wings and making a flatulent snort, all at the same time.

Often accompanying flocks of the relatively tall Little Bustard, especially in winter, is the Pin-tailed Sandgrouse. Extremadura is the one of the best places in

Left: Rocky outcrops such as these provide breeding sites for many of Extremadura's birds of prey, such as vultures and eagles.

Below: The rare Black-bellied Sandgrouse maintains a population of 2,000 pairs in Extremadura.

Above: The Black-winged Kite (this is a juvenile) hunts over the grasslands at dusk by hovering. It often forages at dusk.

Europe to see this declining species, with at least 1,500 individuals present throughout the year here. Found in stonier places, usually at higher elevations (above 1,300m), is its relative, the Black-bellied Sandgrouse, which is slightly more numerous (up to 2,000 birds) but often difficult to see. In Europe it is confined to Iberia. Sandgrouse, which are herbivores, often delay their breeding season here until June, when the first glut of seeds appears in the grasslands.

Other breeding species of the steppe include Common Quail, Montagu's Harrier and Eurasian Stone-curlew, while the air rings in spring with the songs of Greater Short-toed and Calandra Larks, the latter sporting conspicuous black undersides to the wing. Meanwhile, in the winter, as many as 90,000 Common Cranes migrate from northern Europe to spend the winter on nearby agricultural land. These alone would make any visit to Extremadura worthwhile at this time of year but there also happen to be up to 19,000 Greylag Geese and hordes of other wildfowl on the reservoirs and other wetlands.

Another important habitat of Extremadura is known as *dehesa*, a type of open woodland with scattered cork oaks, home to a highly distinctive set of birds. Its signature species is the Black-winged Kite, a very widespread Old World species that is abundant in Africa but very rare in Europe. With its large, forward-facing eyes, this species hunts over tall grass by slowly quartering and hovering, and nests in cork oaks and other low trees. Alongside this species are birds such as European Roller, which relies on ground very rich in large invertebrates, Southern Grey and Woodchat Shrikes, Great Spotted Cuckoo and the localized Iberian Azure-winged Magpie. The cuckoo is a brood parasite of both Eurasian and Iberian

Azure-winged Magpies. The latter often breed in loose colonies and can be seen passing through groves of trees one after the other, each member uttering its shrill calls. Until recently this species was considered conspecific with the Azure-winged Magpie of the Far East and there were suggestions that, in view of the extraordinarily disjunct distribution, the Iberian birds might have been introduced. Recent sub-fossil remains, however, have confirmed that the presence of these subtle blue, pink and black birds is entirely 'natural'.

One of the jewels in the crown of the region of Extremadura is the magnificent Monfragüe National Park, about 60km to the north of Trujillo. This 1,550km² rich mixture of broadleaved forest, scrub and rugged gorges at the confluence of the Rio Tejo and Rio Tietar should be considered as one of the very best sites in Europe for raptors, with some 16 breeding species, including the highest breeding populations in the world of Black Vulture (300 pairs) and Spanish Imperial Eagle

Below: Iberian Azure-winged Magpies live in small groups in the woodlands.

CD tracks

TRACK 7: Great Spotted Cuckoo
TRACK 8: Calandra Lark

(at least 10 pairs, some of which nest on pylons). Egyptian Vultures breed along the gorges, while there is a healthy population of Griffon Vultures (500+ pairs), some of which can be seen at the famous landmark of Penafalcon, a huge rocky outcrop towering over the road into the park. Along with the Spanish Imperial Eagles, Golden, Booted, Bonelli's and Short-toed Eagles all breed, as do Red and Black Kites. On a good day, it is perfectly possible to see every one of these.

The rocky areas such as Penafalcon also hold a range of other exciting species. For many years a pair of Black Storks has bred on the rock, much to the delight of visiting birders, while the supporting cast includes Black-eared Wheatear, Alpine Swift, Red-billed Chough and Blue Rock Thrush, among others. In recent years the very rare (in Europe) White-rumped Swift has also appeared in small numbers, although it usually turns up after most birdwatchers have left the area after the end of May.

Another interesting raptor that occurs in Extremadura is the now globally threatened Lesser Kestrel. This is a species of unusual habits, tending to select towns and buildings in which to nest in colonies, rather than wilder habitats. From its urban base it commutes out over fields and rivers to hunt insects and, occasionally, lizards. Several of the towns in Extremadura have colonies of these birds, including Cáceres and Trujillo, and they often share the rooftops with colonies of White Storks and Pallid Swifts.

It seems that even the towns and villages of Extremadura are great for birds.

Below: Characteristic of rocky areas, the Black Wheatear decorates its nest site with dozens, and sometimes hundreds, of small stones.

Opposite: Europe's 'other' cuckoo, the Great Spotted parasitizes the nests of magpies and crows instead of small birds.

34

Ebro Delta

SITE RANK | 12

HABITAT | Coastal delta with beaches, lagoons and sand bars, plus rice fields, reed swamp, saline steppe, woods

KEY SPECIES | Audouin's, Slender-billed and Mediterranean Gulls, terns, herons including Little Bittern, Collared Pratincole, Kentish Plover

TIME OF YEAR | Excellent all year. Spring and summer best for terns; winter best for wildfowl

Opposite: The Audouin's Gull is arguably the Ebro Delta's most important breeding species, but it hasn't always been so. The colony, the largest in the world, has only been established since 1981.

Lying on the coast of Cataluña in north-east Spain, some 100km north of the metropolis of Barcelona, the Ebro Delta is a wetland of immense importance to birds – indeed, no less than 10 per cent of all the waterfowl in the whole of Spain winter here, which is quite a statistic for such a large and biodiverse country. However, the delta's undoubted status as one of the top sites for birds on the west Mediterranean coast is somewhat overshadowed by the presence of its big brother in the south. The Coto Doñana, the cradle of Spanish birding, is a huge ornithological magnet and will forever draw birders' eyes and longings away from its very impressive rival up here in the underrated north.

But the Cota Doñana does not play host to 15,000 pairs of Audouin's Gull. Nowhere else in the world does, in fact, or even comes close. The figure amounts to about 70 per cent of the world population of this rarity, which is almost confined to the Mediterranean basin as a breeding bird, apart from some on the coast of Morocco. The Audouin's is a specialized hunter that mainly feeds out at sea on pelagic fish such as sardines, which it can snatch from the surface with a dexterous flick of the bill. It often feeds at night to avoid the attentions of the overbearing Yellow-legged Gulls which share its range. In contrast to many other gulls, famed for their opportunism and adaptability, the Audouin's has always been something of a precious species.

Incredibly, the colony on the Ebro Delta has only been in existence since 1981, when 36 pioneering pairs settled down on the tip of the long sandy peninsula on the southern side of the delta, the Punta de la Banya. That they chose this site was a surprise at the time, because almost all the other colonies in the world were on rocky islets. But changes were already afoot in the Audouin's Gull's world. In 1966 it was probably the world's rarest gull, with just 1,000 breeding pairs known, but from that time it began to increase at 10 per cent per annum, the totals boosted by protection of the breeding colonies from disturbance by fishermen and Yellow-legged Gulls. The birds also began to utilize discards from fishing vessels, and at the Ebro, where there was a ready, superabundant supply from the local fleet, the colony increased by some 40 per cent a year. The rate of increase has slowed since but hasn't yet stopped. And the gulls continue to adapt; these days they also forage in the delta's many rice fields, feasting on crayfish.

The Audouin's Gull is perhaps the jewel in the crown of the Ebro Delta's breeding birds but it is not the only highlight. Indeed, it is not even the only gull highlight. There are also some 500 pairs of the smart, elegant Slender-billed Gull

Above: The Ebro Delta hosts Europe's only regular breeding site for the rare Lesser Crested Tern.

here and the habitat is ideal for them, with their preference for shallow, saline waters, where they have the habit of swimming and up-ending like a duck. Other breeding gulls include the ubiquitous Yellow-legged Gull and, at a southern outpost from the rest of their range, a colony of a few hundred pairs of Lesser Black-backed Gull. These birds, and also the terns for which the Ebro is equally famous, use the beaches, dunes and sand spits that punctuate the outer edge of the delta. Jutting out some 20km into the Mediterranean Sea from the nearby coastline and being equally wide where it joins the mainland, the 'triangle' of the delta's shoreline provides plenty of suitable habitat.

The catalogue of terns includes 5,500 pairs of Common Tern, 1,800 pairs of Sandwich Tern, 650 pairs of Little Tern and 300 pairs of Gull-billed Tern, all of which use the beaches and spits. In most years there is a fifth species here too: the Lesser Crested Tern, usually on the Punta del Fangar, a peninsula on the north side of the delta. These are the only regular breeding birds in Europe, although they have also appeared in recent years at the Po Delta, Italy (page 64). The only other colonies in the Mediterranean are on a couple of islands off Libya; the bird is mainly found around the Indian Ocean.

The beach and lagoon areas also attract other birds. On the beaches there is a highly impressive breeding population of Kentish Plover for example (up to 1,500 pairs), while there are usually a few Greater Flamingos present on the lagoons and these have also bred from time to time. The highly scattered Collared Pratincole maintains a population of 70 pairs, mainly on salt flats such as those at La Tancada on the southern edge. From here the birds commute inland to feed on their staple diet, flying insects.

Below: There are 70 pairs of Collared Pratincoles on the Ebro Delta's lagoons and saltings.

The Ebro Delta is very much more than just a marine site. Overall it covers 320km^2, much of which is several kilometres inland from the sea. The whole area is made up from deposits of alluvial soil brought from upstream by the mighty Río Ebro, which cuts the delta into northern and southern halves and ensures that there is a great deal of freshwater too. The major habitat is now rice paddies, which cover more than half of the total area, but there are also many small freshwater pools, canals and marshes, such as those at l'Encanyissada, in the south, which has hides overlooking the site. Between them these areas play host to some highly significant populations of marshland birds. For example, there are thought to be 1,000 breeding Little Bittern here, more than in the Coto Doñana.

Among the many highlights of the freshwater or brackish habitats are 1,500 pairs of Whiskered Tern, 800 pairs of Squacco Heron, 500 pairs of Purple Heron, 1,500 pairs of Red-crested Pochard and no less than 500 pairs of the weird-looking Purple Swamp-hen, which was once a great rarity in Spain but has greatly benefitted from reintroduction schemes. The Ebro birds were introduced from 1990 onwards. Much scarcer but notable breeders include the Glossy Ibis and the Great White Egret, both of which are expanding their ranges in Europe naturally.

As mentioned above, the Ebro Delta holds, if anything, even more birds in the winter than it does in the breeding season. There are, for example, around 75,000 ducks crammed into the area in winter (most of which are Mallard), together with

Right: The smart Black-eared Wheatear is a characteristic inhabitant of rocky and bushy areas.

Above: The Purple Swamp-hen's bizarre appearance masks its range of talents, which include wading, climbing and swimming.

a very impressive 15,000 Eurasian Coot. In recent years a few Red-knobbed Coot have also been reintroduced into the delta, but there are only a handful and searching for them among the multitudes of Eurasian Coot, with the differences between the two so very subtle and small, would probably not rank high as entertainment. The varied habitats of the delta are also excellent for waders and there are some 30,000 of these in the winter, including up to 600 Pied Avocet. And of course there are gulls – lots of them, with 30,000 Mediterranean Gulls a standout figure. Gulls are everywhere in the Ebro.

Finally, mention should be made of the *Riet Vell* project run in the delta by Sociedad Española de Ornitología (SEO) and Birdlife International. In 2001 SEO bought 50ha of rice paddies and formed the *Riet Vell* company to grow and market rice grown in the Ebro under the best organic conditions. It is possible to visit the site on the south of the delta and watch the teeming birds in the paddies and on a freshwater lagoon. It's worth a visit, not just for the birds but to buy the products (rice, pasta and wine) and support the whole enterprise.

CD tracks

TRACK 9: Little Bittern
TRACK 10: Little Tern

40 Organbidexka Col Libre

INFORMATION

SITE RANK | 30

HABITAT | Low mountain pass
(1,440m), forest

KEY SPECIES | Raptors, especially Red
and Black Kites and European Honey-
buzzard; Black and White Storks,
Common Woodpigeon, White-backed
Woodpecker, Lammergeier

TIME OF YEAR | Mainly autumn
migration, July to November, but with
light spring passage and some
interesting resident species

Migration has its hazards, of which the best known are high winds, the danger of ditching into the sea and becoming stranded in the lifeless sands of the Sahara desert. A much less appreciated and understood difficulty lies in a bird's negotiation of mountains and mountain ranges. However, judging by how much individual birds literally go out of their way to avoid the highest peaks, with the latter's potential for dangerous turbulence, sudden cold and extremes of weather, it would seem that the challenges posed by mountains are higher up a bird traveller's agenda than we might think.

One such barrier to migration in Europe is the Pyrenean mountain chain, between France and Spain. In the east, the high peaks reach 3,404m, well above the height at which most birds travel, and are a peril that few dare negotiate. In the west of the range, however, the mountains are very much lower, and a series of north–south mountain passes, or cols, present ideal short cuts for travellers to follow on their way south into Spain. In recent years some of these have become prime ornithological sites, not just for birders but for researchers as well, who are trying to puzzle out the connection between bird movements and the myriad different weather conditions. The most famous of these, with an interesting history as well as a good birding pedigree, is Organbidexka, in the Haute-Soule region of Aquitaine.

Long before birding became a widespread pastime, the locals in this rugged, proud region were well aware of a massive movement of Common Woodpigeons and Stock Doves through their cols in October and November every year. Indeed, they took advantage, setting up shooting points along prominent parts of the pigeons' route. Somewhat resourcefully, they noticed that the birds could be tempted down to land; if the hunters flung small white discs, known as zimbelas, into the air, the pigeons mysteriously landed and could be shot or caught in nets. This pastime became ingrained into Basque culture as la Chasse de la Palombe (the hunt of the woodpigeon).

Over time, what was both a sport and a means of easy food began to take a toll on the migrants. The hunting of birds is very popular in parts of France and Spain, and unfortunately, by modern times, the many north–south-facing cols became littered with small bunkers for shooting – hard to believe in such sophisticated and modern countries. Thousands of pigeons and other migrants, including birds of prey, were also shot indiscriminately and, to the shame of the countries involved, this slaughter continues today. Almost

Left: Mountain ranges such as the Pyrenees form a physical barrier to birds. Most Swallows take the coastal route.

Below: Common Woodpigeons migrate over the area in their millions.

unbelievably, 1,800,000 Common Woodpigeons may die during each season of la Chasse in southern France.

Ironically, therefore, the birds' avoidance of the higher mountains has led them past what has become a much greater peril.

However, in 1979 a small band of ornithologists and conservationists became sickened by the carnage and began, in the face of local opposition from hunters, to rent their own bunker at Organbidexka. They declared it a col libre (hunting-free zone) and began to monitor not just the migration itself but also hunting activities. Just to give an example of what they and the birds are up against, they recorded a total of 25,360 gunshots in a single day in 1982. Nowadays, some 30 years later, the col libre is still in existence and indeed is now the site of a bird observatory. Every year, between August and November, the watch point is staffed by enthusiasts who both monitor the migration and introduce members of the public to the wonders of birds and their movements. In recent years they have added more Pyrenean passes to their list of watch points, including the Col de Lizarrieta, near Ascain, and Lindux, south of St-Jean-Pied-de-Port.

Below: The superb Short-toed Eagle is a regular migrant over the col: about 130 pass over each autumn.

Above: Booted Eagles are quite late migrants, appearing in October. This bird is a pale morph.

It is said that 100,000 pigeons pass the col between late September and November, suggesting that the Pyrenean movement is the largest pigeon passage in Europe and perhaps the world. Interestingly, there is a slight difference in timing: the Stock Doves begin in mid-September, a week or two before the Common Woodpigeons, and they end slightly earlier, at the beginning of November, while the Common Woodpigeons carry on passing until the middle of the month. There is also a smaller movement of Turtle Doves, mainly in September.

Despite its importance for pigeons, Organbidexka has, in recent years, become world famous for its raptor migration. The pass is a bottleneck for raptors avoiding the sea to the west and the higher peaks to the east, while being mountainous enough to enable birds to use updrafts for their journeys. In general, mountain updrafts only exist some 300–400m above the land, so the col is famous for affording quite exceptional low views of many of the passing birds.

The flight begins in mid-August, with the first Black Kites and European Honey-buzzards. These species are the two most numerous here, with averages of 17,209 and 12,354 birds passing each season, often in large flocks. By September the variety increases, with European Honey-buzzards increasing and Black Kites slowing to a trickle, replaced by Montagu's and Western Marsh Harriers (86 and 207 per season respectively), Osprey (138) and Short-toed Eagle (131). There is also a small passage of White and Black Storks, as well as innumerable Barn Swallows. By October the raptor mix has altered slightly and includes what must be one of the largest Red Kite flights in the world (1,721). In this month, Hen Harrier (69), Eurasian Sparrowhawk (324), Common Buzzard (91), Eurasian Hobby (41), Merlin (27) and Common Kestrel (57) pass by in numbers, while, remarkably for this far north, up to about 50 Booted Eagles may also be recorded. October is also excellent for the visible migration of passerines such as larks and pipits, while November signals something of a change, when up to 15,000 Common Cranes

Below: The last movements of the autumn involve Common Cranes. Up to 15,000 may fly over the col during November.

may pass over, in the last migratory flight of the year. In all, some 31,000 migrant raptors use the narrow migration corridor along Organbidexka during the autumn.

Apart from the regular species, it is inevitable that the watch point should record a few oddities, and over the years these have included Egyptian Vulture, Eleonora's Falcon and, bizarrely, one Spanish Imperial Eagle. However, at least 95 per cent of all the raptors seen are European Honey-buzzards and Black Kites.

For birding visitors, the area also offers resident and breeding species such as Lammergeier, White-backed Woodpecker and Iberian Chiffchaff, which breed nearby in the dense forests.

But perhaps the best reason to go to Organbidexka is not so much as a birder but as a human being enjoying the phenomenon of migration. Your presence will add another note of defiance to those whose only interest is in senseless shooting.

Above: It is mainly the broad-winged, soaring birds that use the mountain updrafts for their Pyrenean crossing. This is a White Stork.

CD tracks

TRACK 11: Stock Dove
TRACK 12: Iberian Chiffchaff

46 Lac du Der-Chantecoq

SITE RANK | 24

HABITAT | Large artificial lakes, farmland, meadows, deciduous and coniferous forest

KEY SPECIES | Common Crane, White-tailed Eagle, Great White Egret, Bean and Greater White-fronted Geese, ducks, woodpeckers

TIME OF YEAR | Most popular in winter but excellent all year

There is something unique about this site in a book that attempts to cover the best places for birding in Europe. While a few locations herein are pristine wildernesses and most are superb areas that have been modified by human beings to a greater or lesser extent, the Lac du Der-Chantecoq and its neighbouring reservoirs constitute the sole entry that is completely artificial, having been created by force of human decision and human hand.

This complex of reservoirs in the Champagne region of central France, about 190km south-east of Paris, is also undoubtedly the 'youngest' site covered by the book, having been in existence for less than 50 years. The Lac d'Orient (23km^2) was dug in 1966 in order to store floodwater from the River Seine and was followed in 1990 by the 20km^2 Lac du Temple, just next door; a third reservoir, the 5km^2 Lac d'Amance, which was also constructed in 1990, regulates the River Aube. Meanwhile, a few tens of kilometres to the north, the largest lake of the lot, the 48km^2 Lac du Der-Chantecoq, was constructed in 1974 to hold back water from yet another river, the Marne, in order to prevent spring flooding in Paris. All in all, this massive creation of new freshwater habitat has completely altered the landscape of this sparsely populated, rural part of France, including the drowning of three villages, one of which gives its name, Chantecoq, to the largest lake.

It is not only the landscape that has been altered. Where once there were fields, there is now habitat for ducks, herons and cormorants. Where the ground was dry,

Right: In winter these open, chilly man-made lakes can be desolate places.

there is now habitat for waders and gulls. Tens of thousands of waterbirds use the site in winter and on passage, while in the summer the lakeside marshes provide habitat for breeding species such as Eurasian and Little Bitterns, Gadwall and Purple Heron. Together with its surrounding farmland and rich deciduous and coniferous forest, the area as a whole has become one of the most important birding sites in all of France.

However, no single species has had more impact on birding in this area than the Common Crane. Cranes must always have overflown or rested in the area on migration, but these days, with excellent feeding and roosting conditions available to them, they descend on the area in enormous numbers. It is estimated that almost the entire breeding population of cranes from Scandinavia and nearby Russia stops here on its way to Spain, some 60,000 birds in all. They don't all come at once, especially in the autumn, when the migration period is fairly protracted, but on their return migration in the spring, especially in late February, the birds concentrate in impressive numbers and counts on the roosts on the islands of the Lac du Der-Chantecoq have recorded 25,000 birds. In addition, a few thousand birds remain throughout the winter.

Cranes are marvellously exciting birds, flying with regal, slow wingbeats, moving in neat formations and uttering their extraordinarily loud, atmospheric calls. The far-carrying clanging is made by the elongated trachea, which actually winds

Above: The Common Crane is the area's star bird. The main peaks in numbers occur in February and November.

around the bird's sternum and fuses with it to make a series of plates that vibrate and amplify the sound. The sight and sound of these cranes can be profoundly impressive and on most evenings during the winter there will be birders perched on the western embankment of the lake, waiting for the inbound flight.

Not everybody in the area is a huge crane fan, especially those local farmers who lose large amounts of grain or potatoes to the birds every year. To combat this, a local farm has been acquired, the Ferme des Grues, where the birds can be protected and fed, and where they are entirely welcome; the problem is thus ameliorated, if not entirely solved.

Plenty of other waterbirds can be seen while you are enjoying the sight of the cranes, including a fairly new arrival into the area, the Great White Egret. These stately herons were once very rare in this part of France but at least 30 to 40 now winter annually. In addition, there are plenty of ducks, and many hundreds of the usual common European species can be seen, such as Eurasian Wigeon, Gadwall and Eurasian Teal. Some parts of the lake are deep, so diving ducks turn up regularly, including such scarcities as Smew and Velvet Scoter. Alongside these, there are always some divers and grebes about and the Red-necked Grebe, in particular, is something of a speciality.

Opposite: The woodlands around the lakes, especially Lac d'Orient, are excellent for woodpeckers, although the Grey-headed Woodpecker is extremely hard to find.

Above: Large numbers of Greater White-fronted Geese winter in the area, using the lakes for roosting and the farmland for feeding.

The profusion of wildfowl, and waders too (up to 10,000 Northern Lapwings may be present in winter), is the main attraction for another five-star species. This is the only area in France where White-tailed Eagle regularly winters, and in a good year between three and five individuals may be present. Although surprisingly hard to find in this area, the eagles are always stylish and spectacular, and the pandemonium they can cause to the assembled throng of waterbirds is, in itself, an impressive performance. White-tailed Eagles, despite their enormous size, are surprisingly versatile hunters. Sometimes they will simply scavenge for dead birds or fish, involving a leisurely wander along the shoreline (they have been known to munch on human corpses). At other times they will take to the air, dive down and make a two-footed lunge for a fish just beneath the surface. And for their most exciting, if disturbing, trick they will single out a diving duck, grebe or coot and will make repeated attempts from above to catch it as the poor creature comes up for air. After a few desperate forays beneath the surface, the victim becomes exhausted and is much more easily picked off. It's a cruel example of nature in the raw.

Below: Not many birders come to the lakes of Champagne in the breeding season, but the site holds many excellent birds, including Little Bitterns.

Away from the drama of the lakes, no visitor to the region should overlook the surrounding countryside. The fields and hedgerows are good for species such as Brambling and Great Grey Shrike, while the mature woodlands, especially those around the three southerly lakes, are an excellent draw in themselves. A bit of diligent searching is likely to bag at least five species of woodpecker – Great, Lesser and Middle Spotted, plus European Green and Black – while to see the very scarce Grey-headed requires considerable luck. Other forest birds include Firecrest, Northern Goshawk, Short-toed Treecreeper, Crested Tit and Hawfinch, the latter being a regular visitor to feeding trays in the area, such as at the campground at Larzicourt, on the north of the Lac du Der-Chantecoq. On a slightly different theme, in the winter, Water Pipits, altitudinal migrants from the high meadows of the Central European mountains, feed along the edges of the lakes.

Altogether, 273 species have been recorded in the region as a whole, which, considering that this is more than 250km inland in a temperate area, is a hugely impressive total. And happily, for once, one can reliably report that without the influence of humankind the list would never have begun to approach such dizzy heights.

CD tracks

TRACK 13: Common Crane
TRACK 14: Northern Lapwing

52 # The Camargue

INFORMATION

SITE RANK | 7

HABITAT | Large wetland including reed beds, lagoons and salt pans; limestone semi-desert

KEY SPECIES | Greater Flamingo, Slender-billed Gull, Moustached Warbler, Little Bustard, Pin-tailed Sandgrouse

TIME OF YEAR | Any time, although in midsummer much of the water dries up and crowds of tourists visit

The Camargue, in the south of France, is one of the most famous birding locations in Europe, a huge area (850km^2) of lagoons, marshes, reed swamp, beach, dunes, woodland, gardens and rice paddies. Although it is a fantastic place to visit and an excellent place to dip your feet into southern European birding for the first time, it is also fair to say that it not as good as it once was. The Camargue's quality has been diminishing for years as the toxins of agricultural intensification, rice growing and tourism have gradually eroded its star quality year on year. Nevertheless, it can still teem with birds.

One of Europe's longest rivers, the Rhône, winds its way through Central Europe and tips into the Mediterranean Sea to the west of the city of Marseilles. Just before reaching the sea, it splits into two arms, the Petit Rhône and the Grand Rhône, and between these lies Western Europe's largest river delta. The meandering waterways, myriad sandbars, lagoons and flats, both within the two arms and outside, constitute what we know as the Camargue. It is a romantic and scenic region, steeped in history (the main town, Arles, was originally Roman) and is as famous for its free-ranging white horses and black bulls as it is for its wild animals. To the east, there is a large limestone semi-desert known as La Crau; it is not strictly part of the Camargue but is very close by and is included here for its great ornithological interest.

One of the star attractions for birders in the Camargue is the very large colony of Greater Flamingos, mainly found on the Étang de Fangassier, a large salt pan in the central part of the Camargue, close to the sea. In the late 1960s the flamingos were at risk from the erosion of their nesting islands, so bulldozers were sent in to build new platforms for the birds to use. Since that time the population has more than doubled to nearly 15,000 pairs and the flamingos are regarded as a major tourist attraction. They occur year round, although only a quarter of the population remains during the winter, the rest retreating to Spain and north-west Africa. In recent years these flamingos have been supplementing their normal diet of small invertebrates (from which their pink coloration is derived) with a new food: rice, which is grown locally.

Sharing the shallow saline waters with the flamingos is another pink-flushed bird, the Slender-billed Gull. Indeed, this elegant species is often found feeding at the feet of taller birds, fielding shrimps fleeing oddly shaped bills. This specialized, long-legged gull is one of the few of its family that can run after prey through the water, sometimes gathering in lines to herd fish into the shallows before diving

Left: A typical Camargue landscape, with sumptuous reed swamp providing habitat for large numbers of herons, warblers and rails.

Below: The Greater Flamingo is the Camargue's most famous avian inhabitant. There are no less than 15,000 pairs here and they can be seen all year round.

into the panicking mêlée. This scarce gull began breeding in the Camargue as recently as 1993 and there are now almost 1,000 pairs.

The saline pools suit other specialized birds, too. The Pied Avocet and Black-winged Stilt get their long legs (blue and pink respectively) wet here, either scything their bills through the water (avocet) or picking delicately from the water surface (stilt). Both live up to the name 'wader', being able to use deep, saline water without swimming (although the avocet will swim if necessary). The Kentish Plover, on the other hand, keeps its feet dry, feeding by sight along the sandy edges of the salt pans and lagoons. It also nests on beaches and benefits from being able to run about without the hindrance of stones or vegetation. It maintains a long-legged theme, standing taller than the closely related, shingle-loving Ringed Plover, and it is often seen dashing from place to place, its legs moving too rapidly to be visible, like some mechanical toy.

Another lover of salt water is still an extreme rarity here but could yet become more regular. Given that egrets generally disperse for great distances after

Below: The Camargue attracts a wide range of rarities. The Greater Spotted Eagle, seen most winters, is one of the more regular ones.

breeding, the presence of Western Reef Egrets in the Camargue from time to time, with individual birds often remaining for many years, is perhaps not too surprising: they breed as close as Mauritania and the Red Sea. At the moment these egrets, which are conveniently usually slate-grey, not white, have been recorded 20 or so times in the Camargue, but the habitat here might suit them quite well, especially if the climate becomes hotter, as predicted.

Above: In recent years the Camargue area has hosted a very small but regular wintering population of Pine Buntings.

Above: Moustached Warblers, in contrast to most of their relatives, live in the Camargue's reed beds all year round.

CD tracks

TRACK 15: Greater Flamingo
TRACK 16: Moustached Warbler

Talking of weather, the very best time to visit the Camargue is perhaps during the winter, when the seasonal rains fill up the many ponds and lakes (which are dry between March and September), giving the whole place a lush, verdant look. Wildfowl are everywhere and some impressive numbers have been counted in recent years: 13,000 Gadwall, 23,000 Eurasian Teal and 2,000 Red-crested Pochard, for example, as well as 30,000 Eurasian Coot. This is the season when there can be a notable influx of raptors, including quite a number of rarities or oddities, such as Greater Spotted Eagle, Long-legged Buzzard and Booted Eagle (usually a summer visitor to Europe). The winter period also brings a regular small flock of Pine Buntings, which are usually very rare this far west.

By the spring, many of the breeding wetland birds are confined to the permanent lakes, such as the huge Étang de Vaccarès, effectively a shallow inland sea. This is a great place to see many of Europe's widespread marshland birds, including Purple and Squacco Herons, Western Marsh Harrier, Great Reed Warbler and Bearded Tit. One of the few warblers to winter here is the Moustached Warbler, a bird that is able to pick smaller edible items off marshland vegetation than its competitors can – items that are more reliable year-round food than larger invertebrates. This bird sometimes has eggs in the nest by March.

On the eastern edge of the Camargue National Park, La Crau presents a picture very different from this abundance. It is as flat as the rest of the Camargue but permanently dry, the ground mainly dotted with pebbles and herbs; a few sorry bushes survive here and there. The old delta of the nearby River Durance, it is France's only semi-desert area and holds several species that are rare elsewhere in the country, including a population of several hundred Little Bustards and about 150 Pin-tailed Sandgrouse. These two species often gather together in flocks, since the sandgrouse use the bustards as lookouts. Birders should also look out for European Roller and also the Great Spotted Cuckoo, which uses the local Eurasian Magpie as host. However, both cuckoo and roller can be very difficult to find.

In contrast to the Camargue, most of La Crau is in private hands and therefore has no formal protection. Much is grazed and the amount of habitat available to the special birds diminishes year by year through encroachment by agriculture and irrigation. The future of the sandgrouse, in particular, is threatened, because its population is isolated from others further south in Spain.

Below: The elegant Slender-billed Gull is an expert paddler which thrives in the shallow lagoons.

58 Highlands of Corsica

INFORMATION

SITE RANK | 8

HABITAT | Hill forest, maquis (Mediterranean scrub), mountain tundra, rock faces, streams

KEY SPECIES | Corsican Nuthatch, Corsican Finch, Lammergeier, Alpine Chough, White-winged Snowfinch, Common Crossbill

TIME OF YEAR | All year but spring and summer are best

The island of Corsica, the fourth largest in the Mediterranean, lies just 160km from the French coast, 80km from the Italian coast and 12km from its neighbour Sardinia. Yet its long isolation, beginning five million years ago when the Mediterranean flooded, is reflected in one extraordinary ornithological way – it has its own bird species, found nowhere else in the world. The celebrated Corsican Nuthatch, which dominates the agenda of every birding visitor, has never been seen away from the island, not even in Sardinia. It's the jewel in the crown of the avifauna. And although there is an excellent supporting cast of birds, including a number of highly restricted species and some excellent high-altitude inhabitants, the nuthatch remains the key reason for including Corsica among Europe's best birding locations.

The Corsican Nuthatch was discovered by English naturalist John Whitehead on 12 June 1883, high up in the mountains in a location that he never divulged (he feared that the birds were exceedingly rare and could be wiped out). Having come across his first bird by chance, it took him some considerable time and effort to find another. So began a celebrated birdwatching trend, because the small nuthatches, even today, are still accustomed to giving birders the runaround. They are relatively quiet birds and spend a great deal of time feeding unobtrusively in the upper branches of tall trees on mountain slopes. In common with Whitehead, most people need at least a couple of attempts to find them – but at least their frustrations have historical resonance!

As it happens, Whitehead's fears for his nuthatch were unfounded. The birds are localized but reasonably widespread, occurring from Tartagine in the north to Ospedale in the south, and the world population ranges somewhere between 4,500 and 13,500 pairs. That isn't to say that a casual visitor is likely to run into them. Their distribution is correlated to that of the Corsican Pine (Pinus nigra laricio) along the central mountain chain, mainly at altitudes between 1,000 and 1,500m, and they are most abundant in stands with plenty of old and rotting timber, where they can excavate their own nests and find a good supply of insect food. Engaging to watch, these small, smart nuthatches, with their long, broad white supercilium, frequently make short sallies for flying insects and perform acrobatics at the narrow ends of long branches. They are good value for their star quality.

Once the birding visitor has paid homage to the Corsican Nuthatch, there are plenty of other choice avian targets to find in the Corsican hinterland. Indeed, in recent years the birding appeal of some of these has gone up as taxonomists have reassessed the status of some of the distinctive forms found on Corsica and Sardinia. Their most significant pronouncements have concerned the island version of the Citril Finch. On the mainland this species is only found in upland areas above 700m (at least when breeding) but on Corsica and Sardinia it can be found at sea level up to 1,650m. It also looks different from the continental form, with a warm brown (not grey) back and a brighter yellow breast, and it sounds different too, so, all in all, most authorities now consider it to be a separate species from the Citril Finch. It is known as Corsican Finch and is common on the island.

Other interest has recently concerned the warblers in the genus *Sylvia*. Now that the Balearic version of the dark-plumaged Marmora's Warbler is frequently assumed to be separate, that means that the birds found on Corsica, Sardinia and Elba are also breeding endemics (some winter in North Africa). There has also been interest in the local Subalpine Warbler (shared with the nearby Italian coast), which has a different call and is evidently genetically distinct from nearby

Above: One of Corsica's many specialities is the Marmora's Warbler, which lives in the maquis.

Below: Corsica is very mountainous, and could be seen as a southern extension of the Alps.

Above: A sure sign of Corsica's highland credentials is the presence of White-winged Snowfinch, although it is rare.

Opposite: The mountains of Corsica hold a small but significant population of Lammergeiers.

populations, so you could say that the warblers of Corsica live in something of a hotbed of taxonomic intrigue. Who knows how many new species will be declared in the future.

The warblers are denizens of one of Corsica's most important habitats, Mediterranean maquis, which covers some 43 per cent of the island. The term maquis comes from the Corsican word macchia, meaning scrubland; this biome typically consists of densely growing evergreen shrubs such as holm oak, tree heath, strawberry tree, sage, juniper, buckthorn, spurge olive and myrtle. The habitat is full of various aromatic plants, and visitors to Corsica can be overwhelmed by the pleasing scents of the countryside. Birders would expect to find plenty of warblers in any habitat with thick vegetation and, in addition to the ones mentioned above, there are also Dartford and Sardinian Warblers. Other common maquis inhabitants include the Corsican Finch, Red-backed Shrike and Cirl Bunting.

Above: The truly montane Alpine Chough occurs on Corsica in the absence of its close relative, the Red-billed Chough.

CD tracks

TRACK 17: Corsican Finch
TRACK 18: Corsican Nuthatch

At this stage it is worth mentioning that, in addition to its range of specialities, Corsica also offers a sprinkling of what might be termed 'oddities'. These are birds that might not be expected on the mainland but occur here, and vice versa. Thus, for example, there are no House Sparrows, but Italian Sparrows (now recognized as a separate species) occur instead, and in place of the Common Starling is a large population of Spotless Starlings (really an Iberian speciality). The common crow is the Hooded rather than the Carrion Crow. These everyday species all help to give the island a distinctive ornithological profile.

One of the outstanding features of Corsica, as any visitor will tell you, lies in its extraordinary topography. This island is definitively mountainous; there are 20 peaks above 2,000m, with the highest, Monte Cinto, at 2,706m, which happens to be only 25km from the sea. Rather than resembling the gently hilly French coast, the island is more accurately considered as a southern extension of the Alps, and it is not surprising that many of the best birds are associated with upland habitats.

On the slopes of the hills, particularly below 1,500m, much of the area is blanketed by forest. This includes both deciduous forest, of oak, chestnut and beech, and pine and fir forests, the latter dominating higher up. In these woodlands occur birds that typically abound in temperate climates, including the Eurasian Treecreeper, which replaces the Short-toed Treecreeper here, and such birds as Coal Tit, Long-tailed Tit, Great Spotted Woodpecker, Northern Goshawk, Goldcrest and Firecrest. Something of a speciality here is the Common Crossbill, which, yet again, represents an unusual form, with a broader bill than the nearby mainland birds. It is confined, like the Corsican Nuthatch, to south-facing Corsican Pine forests.

Further up a suite of specialists occur on the rocks and alpine tundra. If ever an area needed an endorsement of its high-altitude credentials, one of these, the Alpine Chough, provides it. This species almost never descends below 1,500m throughout its range and has been recorded living and feeding higher in altitude (8,235m) than any other bird in the world (in the Himalayas). It is reasonably common in Corsica's central spine and occurs here without the closely related Red-billed Chough, which is absent from the island.

Other high-altitude and 'rocky' species found widely on Corsica include the Water Pipit, Alpine Accentor, Northern Wheatear, Golden Eagle, Rufous-tailed and Blue Rock Thrushes, Rock Sparrow, Crag Martin and Alpine Swift, while Dipper and Grey Wagtail inhabit the fast-flowing mountain streams. Three other montane species are uncommon: Lammergeier, Wallcreeper and White-winged Snowfinch. The Wallcreeper does breed in small numbers but is primarily a winter visitor and can be found on the many tall sea cliffs at this season, as well as in the mountains. The White-winged Snowfinch seems confined to the area around Monte Cinto, while the Lammergeier maintains a precious foothold on the island of perhaps eight pairs. It is, though, the sort of bird that elevates Corsica from a very good mountain site into an outstanding one.

Left: There's no doubt about the identity of Corsica's star bird – the endemic Corsican Nuthatch, which was first discovered in 1883.

64 Po Delta

INFORMATION

SITE RANK | 25

HABITAT | Beaches, coastal lagoons, salt marsh, freshwater lakes and marshes, woodland

KEY SPECIES | Pygmy Cormorant, herons, Glossy Ibis, Greater Flamingo, Ferruginous Duck, Red-crested Pochard, Collared Pratincole, Mediterranean and Slender-billed Gulls, terns including Gull-billed and Whiskered, Little Crake

TIME OF YEAR | All year round

Italy's Po Delta region is one of Europe's best-kept birdwatching secrets. Situated in the north-east of the country, on the Adriatic Coast, it is of vital importance for all sorts of breeding, passage and wintering birds, so it is a classic site throughout the year. Over 50,000 waterbirds use the site in winter, while several species of gulls and terns reach into the thousands of breeding pairs. Irresistibly for those with wider interests, the delta also happens to span the gap between two of Italy's most fabulous cultural centres, world-famous Venice to the north and the smaller, picturesque and underrated Ravenna to the south. Thus it is a good destination to visit in order to share pastimes, and the birding half will most certainly not be disappointed.

Although a great deal of the delta has been built over and strung with canals and dykes over the years, there is still plenty of superb 'wild' habitat left, especially for wetland birds. In 1988 the area was declared a regional park, covering some 591km^2, and since that time has been adapted for all sorts of tourist interests, including birdwatching. There are dozens of excellent walks and loops that are easily followed into the best areas, many fitted with hides or raised platforms, making the birdwatching easy. In Italy, where birds have been traditionally shot rather than watched, the facilities and provisions for birding represent a significant shift in people's attitudes; the sport of hunting is no longer widely supported, although not many of the locals yet go birding themselves. Inspired by places like the Po Delta, this could quickly change.

At first sight this can be a bewilderingly big area to work but there are plenty of reserves within the delta area where birders can focus their attention. In the northern stretch, for example, nearest to Venice, a large arm of the sea, the Sacca di Gor, is a superb place for resting and roosting gulls, including Slender-billed and Mediterranean Gull, and Gull-billed Tern. Nearby is the large brackish lagoon of Valle Bertuzzi, where Black-winged Stilts and Mediterranean Gulls nest on the salt flats, and the adjacent reed beds hold such species as Purple Heron and Great White Egret, which actually occur widely. In all, the Po Delta is by far the most important breeding site in Italy for herons and one of the most important in Europe.

Further south there is another gem of a place, the Valli di Cammachio, a huge complex of lagoons (the largest in Italy) and nearby salt marshes that simply teem with birds. Italy's largest colony of Greater Flamingos (nearly 1,000 pairs) is found here, along with its only colony of Eurasian Spoonbills. Other breeding

Left: The Eurasian Spoonbill thrives in the Valli di Commachio, nesting in trees and wading in the shallows, using its sensitive bill to detect prey.

Above: Not your average tern, the Gull-billed Tern feeds on insects and even lizards as well as fish.

species include Kentish Plover (maximum 100 pairs), Mediterranean Gull (nearly 2,000 pairs), Gull-billed, Common, Sandwich and Little Terns and Collared Pratincole. At Boscoforte, on a small peninsula that juts out into the giant lagoon, there have been nesting attempts by the very rare Lesser Crested Tern, among the more numerous species. In the many reed beds surrounding the lagoons are significant numbers of Eurasian Bittern, Purple Heron, Western Marsh Harrier and Great Reed Warbler, while the breeding wildfowl of the area include Common Shelduck, Gadwall and Garganey. Montagu's Harriers nest in the surrounding fields.

The Worldwide Fund for Nature reserve at Punte Alburete represents something of a change of scene. In contrast to all the open lagoons and salt marshes in the northern part of the delta, this reserve protects a small area of flooded forest made up of willow and ash trees, home to, among other attractions, Italy's only colony of Pygmy Cormorants. The 2km route around the reserve also takes in reed beds and meadows, and overall this is one of the richest sites for birding in the whole delta. The roll-call of herons is especially impressive, with Purple, Black-crowned Night and Squacco Herons and Great White Egrets all breeding, along with Little and Eurasian Bitterns. There is also a colony of Glossy Ibis. Ducks are

Opposite: A Great White Egret shows off its impressive breeding plumes.

Below: Punte Alburete hosts Italy's only breeding colony of Pygmy Cormorants. This image shows an adult (left) and a juvenile.

well represented, with scarcer species such as Ferruginous Duck and Red-crested Pochard usually present in the fresh water.

South again and the saltwater, or at least brackish, theme returns, with the lagoons at Pialassa della Baiona and Pololonga supporting one of the best gull breeding sites in the delta: Black-headed, Mediterranean and Slender-billed Gulls nest here on specially constructed islands, along with Common, Little and Gull-billed Terns. The same species also occur not far away at the southern edge of the delta, at the Cervia salt pans, together with large numbers of Yellow-legged Gulls (some 16,000 pairs have been counted). These huge salt pans, which date back at least to the time of the Romans, are still working today, and while the extreme salinity restricts the number of species using the waters, the pans are much appreciated by Pied Avocets and Black-winged Stilts, while Kentish Plovers breed on the bare surrounding sand. Outside the breeding season, the salt pans attract

Below: A Glossy Ibis lives up to its name. The shallow waters of the Po Delta make ideal habitat for long-legged wading birds.

Greater Flamingos and large numbers of waders, including Dunlin and Ruff, and wildfowl such as Eurasian Wigeon.

Finally, some 30km inland, near the town of Argenta but still within the regional park, the scene changes once again. The delightful Valle Santa reserve encompasses a freshwater lagoon skirted by wet meadows. Both Spotted and Little Crakes breed in the reed beds here, while Whiskered Terns nest on the water lilies and Penduline Tits frequent patches of willow scrub. Very different in character from most of the rest of the delta, it demonstrates the exciting and diverse range of habitats that occur in this part of what is, ornithologically, largely a neglected country.

Above: The smart Mediterranean Gull breeds on some of the delta's lagoons. It feeds mainly on insects in the summer.

CD track

TRACK 19: Zitting Cisticola
TRACK 20: Whiskered Tern

Lesvos

INFORMATION

SITE RANK | 3

HABITAT | An island with olive groves, scrubby hillsides, conifer woodlands and small marshes and other wetlands

KEY SPECIES | Migrants, Krüper's and Western Rock Nuthatches, Rüppell's Warbler, Cinereous and Cretzschmar's Buntings, Chukar, Eleonora's Falcon, Masked Shrike

TIME OF YEAR | Best in passage periods, especially mid-April to mid-May and again in September and October

There can be few easier and more relaxing places to witness great birding in Europe than on the Greek island of Lesvos. Situated just off the coast of Turkey in the eastern Aegean, Lesvos is a travelling hub in more ways than one. It is on the Mediterranean tourist trail, offering good connections, decent hotels and all the usual facilities expected by northern Europeans in search of reliable Mediterranean sun. Secondly and more importantly, however, it is also on a major migration route, part of the Eurasian–East African flyway, used by hundreds of thousands of birds annually during their intercontinental travels. The combination of comfort for viewing mixed with the chance of seeing some sensational migratory movement within a relatively small area (the island covers 1,632km^2) makes Lesvos one of the most popular destinations in all of Europe for birders in holiday mood. In the busiest season (late April and early May), binocular-clad huddles turn up almost everywhere.

Most visitors stay in the town of Kalloni, in the central north of the island, ensuring that they are right on top of some of the best sites available. The Kalloni salt pans, for example, are an easy walk from the accommodation, making the traditional pre-breakfast wanders some of the most productive and enjoyable parts of any week here. Indeed, throughout the island, few birds are far away from a charming taverna, and vice versa. Most groups keep to a relaxed schedule.

As far as birds are concerned, the sheer unpredictability of migratory movement is perhaps the island's most enduring delight, especially for the growing army of repeat visitors. Day to day, the current weather and the recent weather determines what might turn up: clear weather for raptors, frontal systems for passerines and waterbirds, and so on. Northerly winds in spring are especially useful, because, once they relent, birds will arrive in streams, as if a dam has broken. However, every year is different; for example, 2009 was a poor year for waders, put off by the high levels of water from the previous winter. And the birds themselves are forever fickle: some years produce large flocks of Glossy Ibis and marsh terns, while others produce small numbers; some years are good for White Pelicans, others not. As an example, 2009 was a poor year for raptors, with hardly any Montagu's Harriers and Levant Sparrowhawks, while it was generally good for terns and certain smaller migrants, such as Wryneck, Icterine Warbler and Citrine Wagtail.

However, now that Lesvos has been a birding destination for some 25 years, a little of the unpredictability has been remoulded into experience. Some spots – or,

Left: The splendid Rüppell's Warbler is a speciality of extreme south-east Europe, but has become rare on the island.

Above: The island of Lesvos lies on a major migration route. The widest range of species occurs in the spring.

indeed, birds – are so well known that tour groups effectively make pilgrimages to see certain species at certain sites. For example, Metochi 'Lake' (actually a widening of the Christou River) in the centre north of the island is everybody's stake-out for rails and crakes, especially Little Crake. In spring, a handful of these elusive birds, which are difficult to see almost everywhere in Europe, can usually be spotted skulking at the base of the reed stems here (they are highly aquatic and frequent swimmers), and they are sometimes accompanied by mud-hugging

Baillon's and Spotted Crakes too. At the same time, the area around the Kalloni salt pans is usually the best area to look for passing Pallid and Montagu's Harriers, while Ipsilou Monastery in the west is one of the very best areas for migrant passerines (especially flycatchers, warblers and chats) and passing swifts (including Alpine and Pallid). Similar rules apply to the breeding birds, some of which, for example Rüppell's Warbler, are highly localized. The growing body of local knowledge is such that it is now quite difficult to have a bad week here.

There is a cultural element to birding in Lesvos. Most visitors come from the west, from Britain, Holland, Sweden and Germany, and, as such, these enthusiasts will usually already be familiar with the birds and sites of the western side of Europe, in France, Spain and Italy, for example. Lesvos offers the eastern equivalent, where birders finally dip their toes into the avifauna of Eastern Europe, experiencing the delight of seeing such birds as White-winged Black Tern, Temminck's Stint, Wood Sandpiper, Ortolan Bunting, Thrush Nightingale and Red-footed Falcon for the first time. Until recently, when it became genuinely easy to 'do' such countries as Hungary, Romania and Bulgaria, Lesvos provided an easy way to enjoy the eastern birds on their migratory travels.

Opposite: Every visitor to Lesvos want to see the Krüper's Nuthatch, here at its only station in Europe.

Below: The Eleonora's Falcon is a regular passage migrant in spring and autumn.

Lesvos is, incidentally, mainly a spring destination. Although plenty of birds do pass through in autumn, they don't do so in the numbers that appear in April and May. As far as passerines are concerned, many leave their breeding areas early and have moved south in July or August, leaving the traditional autumn months a little quiet. There are still plenty of birds around but many fewer bird tours visit at this time.

Although the island is most famous for its passage birds, they are not the only attractions on the island. Given Lesvos's location close to the mainland of Turkey and distant from the rest of Greece, it is not surprising that there are several breeding species of more eastern origin. The most sought after is the diminutive Krüper's Nuthatch, here in its only European station. About 600 pairs breed in the northern and eastern side of the island, in woods of Turkish Pine (Pinus brutia) up to an altitude of 800m, where the birds spend much of their time feeding high up in the canopy. These birds feed on insects in the summer but seeds in the winter and, because the cones of Turkish Pine close in wet weather, they have to cache the latter when conditions are good. These are not the only nuthatches in Lesvos. In more exposed habitats the Western Rock Nuthatch is common. And while the

Below: Another of the specialities found on Lesvos, the Cinereous Bunting is easier to see here than anywhere else in Europe.

Krüper's Nuthatch nests in holes in trees, this species places a remarkable flask-shaped structure made up from mud, animal dung and insect parts into a rock face, often quite close to the ground.

Another highly sought-after rarity is the Cinereous Bunting, a soberly clad species washed with subtle grey except for a dash of lemon-yellow on the head. This species is not entirely confined in Europe to Lesvos, because a few pairs occur in other parts of Greece, but the 250 or so pairs do make up the bulk of the European breeding population. It occurs in the arid west and north of the island, in open areas with low scrub and boulders.

Apart from these two main draws, several other breeding birds of Europe's south-eastern extremity also occur on Lesvos, including the handsome Rüppell's Warbler (now very rare, with only three pairs remaining), Chukar, Olive-tree Warbler, Isabelline Wheatear and Black-headed and Cretzschmar's Buntings. The White-throated Robin, another eastern speciality that breeds in central Turkey, has recently been recorded breeding but is not thought to be regular here.

With birds like this, and plenty of time to enjoy them, it is little wonder that Lesvos draws the crowds.

Above: Recent years have seen an upsurge in the number of records of Citrine Wagtails.

CD tracks

TRACK 21: Krüper's Nuthatch
TRACK 22: Cretzschmar's Bunting

76 Dadia Forest

SITE RANK | 26

HABITAT | Open forest composed of oak, pine and beech, together with gorges, agriculture, grassland and rivers

KEY SPECIES | Black, Egyptian and Griffon Vultures, Short-toed Eagle, Lesser Spotted Eagle, Eastern Imperial Eagle

TIME OF YEAR | Birds of prey are present all year but late spring through to autumn is the best time

What's the best site for raptors in Europe? You might expect it to be Falsterbo, or Gibraltar, perhaps, each of which shows off the spectacle of migrating birds passing over in spring and autumn. But if it is sheer species diversity that counts rather than total numbers, or more simply the high number of breeding species, it is actually Greece's Dadia Forest that comes out on top. An astonishing 21 species of day-flying birds of prey breed here with some regularity and no less than 36 species have been recorded in all, most of them annually. It's a remarkable statistic for a location that is still not among the most famous of birding names on our continent.

The Dadia Forest, or, to give it its full name, the Dadia–Lefkimi–Soufli Forest, is situated in the extreme east of Greece, close to the border with Bulgaria and Turkey. Long used as a hunting hideaway, it was first officially protected in 1980 after intense lobbying from conservation agencies; it was designated as a National Park in 2006. It now covers a total area of 42,370ha, 7,290ha of which is designated as a high-protection zone, where disturbance is not allowed. Outside the protected area are a few small, traditional rural settlements and many small farm plots. Within the forest, the main trees are oaks and pines, with stands of beech here and there, giving the forest rather more of a Central European than a Mediterranean feel.

Right: The most famous residents of Dadia Forest are the Black Vultures. They visit the area's feeding stations every day.

Above: The Eastern Imperial Eagle used to breed in the area, and there are high hopes that it will do so again. This is an immature.

The diversity of raptors here is exceptional. This is partly due to its location in the south-east of Europe and partly due to the varied landscape. It is not simply a large, closed forest. Far from it – the forested sections are rather open, with a shrubby understorey, and there are plenty of clearings and patches of lightly farmed land, which make ideal hunting places for many birds of prey. At the same time, tall trees in undisturbed patches of forest, together with plenty of cliffs and rocky outcrops, make good, secretive nest sites. So, for example, the needs of such birds as the European Honey-buzzard or Levant Sparrowhawk, which prefer deep forest, are served at the same time as those of the Lesser Spotted Eagle and the Common Kestrel, which habitually hunt over open country and nest on the woodland edge.

The most recent counts of breeding raptors are extraordinary. For example, it is estimated that there are about 350 territories in the park overall and these include such numbers as 120 pairs of Common Buzzard, 25 pairs of European Honey-buzzard, up to 20 pairs of Lesser Spotted Eagle, 10 pairs of Booted Eagle, up to 20 pairs of Northern Goshawk and 30 pairs of Eurasian Sparrowhawk. A particularly impressive statistic is the 35–40 pairs of Short-toed Eagle, a testament

Above: Among the supporting cast to the raptor-fest is the Western Rock Nuthatch, which occurs on the slopes and cliffs.

Right: The Olive-tree Warbler is another of the south-east European specialities that occurs in the area. Note the pale wing-panel.

to the highly impressive reptile and amphibian fauna, which itself amounts to 40 species (and also provides most of the food for the local Lesser Spotted Eagles). These large birds are snake specialists and their breeding sites have been carefully studied at Dadia; the ideal location is in a tall tree a long way from human disturbance, on the upper third of a south-facing slope, close to clearings and within range of a rainwater gully or other watercourse. It is a tribute to the richness and size of this site that such specifications can be matched so often.

Less numerous breeding species at Dadia include some specialities of south-east Europe, including 4–5 pairs of Levant Sparrowhawk (which here are lizard specialists) and 2–3 pairs of Long-legged Buzzard, plus more widespread birds such as Golden Eagle, Common Kestrel, Hobby, and Lanner and Peregrine Falcons. The globally threatened Eastern Imperial Eagle used to breed but has ceased to do so; nevertheless, several young birds are present each summer in the area and there are high hopes that they will begin to settle down again soon. As an extra attraction to bird of prey buffs, in late summer and autumn, species such as Red-footed and Eleonora's Falcons, Steppe Eagle and harriers can also be seen passing by in addition to the roll-call of breeding species.

Exciting though all of these species are, the true flagship of the Dadia Forest National Park is actually the Black Vulture. This huge scavenging bird, with the largest and most powerful bill of any European vulture (it can open tough hides that cannot be pierced by Griffons), is now found nowhere else in the Balkan region and is fast declining almost everywhere it occurs. In the forests in this corner of Greece, however, there are about 100 individuals present all year and each season about 20–25 pairs breeding, maintaining a precious healthy population. It is one of three vulture species here. There are 7–13 pairs of Egyptian Vulture in the park, each of which selects its own cliff nest site, while Griffon Vultures breed nearby in colonies on cliff tops. The Black Vultures build their nests in the treetops and space their nests fairly well apart.

In order to help the vultures, the authorities have set up a permanent feeding station near the peak of Gibrena (620m), where carcasses are placed regularly to provide a source of food for them (and there are plans for another two feeding stations). A hide has been built 600m away and this, at present, together with the nearby park headquarters, forms the ecotourism hub of Dadia National Park. The Ecotourist Centre of Dadia is extremely well run and maintained (with finance from the Worldwide Fund for Nature, the EU and the Prefecture of Evros), with everything from video presentations on the birds to the provision of a minibus service from the HQ to the observatory and the use of telescopes and binoculars free to visitors. It is possible to stay here too. In such an important area it is heartening to experience the commitment to the wildlife.

Below: Visitors looking for raptors might be distracted by passerine specialities such as the Sombre Tit.

Opposite: The Semicollared Flycatcher benefits from the mixture of oak, pine and beech forests which are found at Dadia.

Although it is always worth visiting the observatory, where there are usually vultures and eagles around (Golden and Lesser Spotted Eagles, with the addition of Greater Spotted Eagle during the winter), this whole area calls out for walks along the many tracks and slow, patient scans from the various watchpoints. Birds of prey don't tend to come out of hiding all at once, so a stay of several days will be needed to see most of the species, especially the more elusive ones such as the Goshawk, Levant Sparrowhawk and European Honey-buzzard.

Although the Dadia Forest is overwhelmingly a bird of prey site, there will be plenty of other birds around to form an impressive supporting cast for the visiting birder. These will include a range of south-eastern European species, such as Chukar (one of the few places in Europe where this bird occurs), Olive-tree and Eastern Olivaceous Warblers, Lesser Grey and Masked Shrikes, Semicollared Flycatcher, Western Rock Nuthatch, Sombre Tit and Black-headed Bunting. It's enough to make you take your eyes away from black dots in the sky.

82

Black Sea Coast

INFORMATION

SITE RANK | 20

HABITAT | A large area with a variety of habitats including sea cliffs, coastal and freshwater wetlands, forest and farmland

KEY SPECIES | Paddyfield Warbler, Pied and Isabelline Wheatears, Semicollared Flycatcher, Dalmatian Pelican, Levant Sparrowhawk, migrants

TIME OF YEAR | Good all year round but exceptional in passage periods (March to May and August to October)

The Black Sea coast of Bulgaria is a large site but a singular marvel. The entire coastline from Durankulak in the north to Ropotamo in the south is part of the same birding motorway, the 'Via Pontica', which funnels millions of travelling birds between their breeding grounds in western Eurasia and the migratory bottlenecks of the eastern Mediterranean, the gateway to the African continent. The various sites along this coast are therefore merely different rest areas along the same jammed thoroughfare, and in spring or autumn you might, in theory, encounter the same individual birds at different points of their journey. If you mix this migratory phenomenon in with a very impressive variety of breeding birds, many of them extremely scarce in Europe, plus a sprinkling of wintering star species, then you have concocted a recipe for some of the most exciting birding that can be experienced anywhere in Europe.

Although the area is superb throughout the year, most birders come to Bulgaria during the peak migration months, and no wonder – just about every type of migrant uses the Via Pontica. Thus, while birding the Black Sea coast in spring or autumn you might experience an overnight fall of small passerines, such as flycatchers, warblers and chats, one morning in your hotel grounds, while a few hours later calm conditions might induce a movement of raptors, storks or pelicans overhead. Offshore, inclement weather may see a movement of gulls, terns and Yelkouan Shearwaters, while a settled period will see a day by day change in the constituent waders at one of the many lagoons or beaches and warblers in the bushes. Different meteorological conditions bring different birds and, as an observer, it seems that you cannot lose. There are always large numbers of birds around throughout this region and thus, in a couple of weeks in May or September, it is hard not to accrue a list of 170 or more species.

A good example of this richness is found at Lake Atanasovsko. No less than 316 species have been recorded in this complex of salt pans close to the large industrial town of Burgas and part of the area is designated as a Ramsar site of international importance – astonishing since it is both a working industrial site and a bit of an eyesore. In a single autumn over 37,000 Great White Pelicans have been counted passing through or over the lake, together with 2,000 or more Dalmatian Pelicans, 23,000 European Honey-buzzards, 200,000 White Storks, 30,000 Common Buzzards, 25,000 Lesser Spotted Eagles and 4,500 Black Storks. These impressive numbers have a notable supporting cast, including significant numbers of such birds as Red-footed Falcon, Levant Sparrowhawk, Booted and

Short-toed Eagles, Glossy Ibis, Eurasian Spoonbill and Pygmy Cormorant. And that's not to mention the waders: Red-necked Phalarope, Marsh, Broad-billed and Curlew Sandpipers, and Temminck's Stint are all regular and the latter two may turn up in tens or even hundreds. Other migrants include Little Crake, Bluethroat, Ruddy Shelduck, Yellow and Citrine Wagtails, various herons and a host of warblers but, to be honest, almost anything could turn up here. Although not all coastal wetlands are as rich as this one, Lake Atanasovsko offers a range of species on migration typical of similar sites all along the coast.

While the Bulgarian Black Sea coast has several notable wetlands, two of the most interesting sites for migratory birds are in fact headlands: Cape Kaliakra, north of Varna, and Cape Emine, between Varna and Burgas. Both jut out a couple of kilometres from the surrounding land and, as a result, form bottlenecks that concentrate migratory birds. Of the two, Cape Kaliakra is the most impressive but both can be spectacular; even if there aren't many birds around, their 60m-high cliffs and sea views are worth the effort to visit. And while many of the birds are the same as those seen at the wetlands, including pelicans, raptors and storks passing over, these areas have the advantage of more exciting seawatching and better falls of passerine migrants. For example, birds that pass by over the sea include Yelkouan Shearwaters (the eastern Mediterranean and Black Sea endemic), a range of gulls including Slender-billed, many terns and, later in the season, grebes and divers. The bushes and shrubs along both capes can, at times

Above: Cape Kaliakra is a superb site for migrants and for breeding species such as Pied and Isabelline Wheatears. It almost befits a chapter of its own.

Right: The splendid Black-headed Bunting is a common breeding bird in Bulgaria.

(mainly following inclement conditions), be alive with an impressive range of warblers, chats and flycatchers. In particular, Red-breasted Flycatchers can be everywhere.

Cape Kaliakra is far from just a migratory watch point; it also boasts a wealth of exciting breeding species. The ground running up to the cape includes a remnant of steppe vegetation and here the rare Isabelline Wheatear breeds in one of its only stations in Europe. This leggy, plain-plumaged wheatear differs from the Northern Wheatear in being more ground-hugging and making longer runs between stops for scanning; it usually nests in rodent holes. It shares the bare ground with Calandra and Short-toed Larks, Eurasian Stone-curlew and Tawny Pipit. Another extremely scarce steppe species, the Saker Falcon, also sometimes occurs here.

You might think that one rare wheatear might be enough for any European site but rocky areas on the Black Sea coast of Bulgaria, including Kaliakra, also boast a small population of Pied Wheatear, a species which is also, like the Isabelline, mainly found outside Europe. Closely related to the Black-eared Wheatear and essentially its eastern equivalent, the Pied Wheatear hunts mainly by watching from a low perch up to 1m above short grass and diving down to catch any invertebrates spotted. It nests beneath stones, in walls or in rock piles and is found on cliffs, rocky outcrops and generally quite desolate areas.

A quite different speciality is found in marshes in the very north of Bulgaria, with Lake Durankulak being the best-known site. This is the Paddyfield Warbler, an Asian species which is really a specialist of forest-steppe lakes much further to the east and is on the very edge of its range here. It tends to prefer small lakes and hugs low vegetation on the edge of reed beds rather than the ranks of reeds themselves but otherwise is ecologically similar to the Reed Warbler.

Further south-eastern specialities abound, although they might not be as rare in Europe as those mentioned above. Bulgaria has good populations of Semicollared Flycatcher, a globally near-threatened species only fairly recently recognized as distinct from Pied and Collared Flycatchers. It spends more time in

Below: The boldly patterned Pied Wheatear's main breeding range is in Asia, but it has a small foothold on the Black Sea coast of Bulgaria.

Above: Calandra Larks are conspicuous breeding birds in steppe country.

Opposite: The Paddyfield Warbler is most abundant on the steppe lakes of Central Asia. It is rare in Europe, and mainly found in reed beds within sight of the Black Sea coast.

CD tracks

TRACK 25: Paddyfield Warbler
TRACK 26: Lesser Grey Shrike

the canopy making aerial sallies than the Pied Flycatcher and rarely seems to visit the ground, as the other species will. It inhabits oak and beech forests in hilly areas. Other south-eastern birds include the Olive-tree Warbler (Kaliakra is a good site for this tricky species), Ferruginous Duck (Durankulak), Red-footed Falcon, Long-legged Buzzard, Syrian Woodpecker, Sombre Tit, Lesser Grey and Masked Shrikes and the gloriously plump and colourful Black-headed Bunting.

Finally, the birding highlights on the Black Sea coast don't all disappear with the summer and autumn, for winter also brings some spectacular birding, mainly to the wetlands. Lake Atanasovsko and Lake Burgas, for instance, play host to such species as Dalmatian Pelican, Pygmy Cormorant, Great White Egret and White-tailed Eagle, while there are also a few White-headed Ducks, a threatened species, at both sites. But the real excitement of Bulgaria in winter is the geese: indeed, some tour companies run special trips to see them. Between November and February up to 60,000 Red-breasted Geese winter in the north, around Durankulak and the Sabla wetlands, feeding on the surrounding dry farmland and roosting on the marshes. Alongside these are a few Lesser White-fronted Geese, another species that specializes on feeding on steppe-like grassland, plus large numbers of Greater White-fronted and a few Barnacle and Bean Geese. Mid-February is the peak time to go to see them.

88 Danube Delta

There are many who consider this to be quite simply the finest site for birds in the whole of Europe and it would be difficult to disagree. It certainly has some measurable superlatives; it is, for example, the largest continuous marshland in Europe and has an authentic claim to the largest expanse of reed beds in the entire world. Within its core area of 733km^2 there are extraordinary and scarcely rivalled numbers of breeding birds: 2,500 pairs of Pygmy Cormorant and Great White Pelican, 3,000 pairs of Black-crowned Night Heron, 2,000 pairs of Squacco Heron, 1,500 pairs of Glossy Ibis and 20,000 pairs of Whiskered Tern. And these are only a few of the 176 or so species that have been recorded breeding here. This truly is one of the great refuges for birds in the European continent.

The delta forms where the Danube, after flowing for 2,860km, splits into three main branches – the Chilia, Sulina and Sfantu Gheorghe Rivers – while still 90km from the Black Sea. Between these rivers lies a dense network of interconnecting channels with a remarkable combined length of 3,500km. Within this maze the main habitat type is reed swamp but there are also areas of lake, sand dunes, scrub, woodland and meadow. One peculiar characteristic of the delta is the existence of 'plaurs', islets formed by decaying reed debris built up over the years to 1–1.6m in height. The plaurs float and their position changes constantly according to the conditions of wind and current. Another local feature is the 'grind', a sand dune system; many of the site's more substantial woodlands grow on these.

The only way to explore the delta is by boat, and on the Romanian side ecotourism is well advanced, with 'floating hotels' set up to cater for wildlife watchers (go in a group, though, because these are very expensive to charter). Some of these are luxurious and the whole adventure can feel like a cruise. From the moment you leave port you are immediately plunged into a quite different world from the one you left, where reeds grow as far as the eye can see, the pace is slower and the wildlife holds sway. The abundance of birds in spring or summer is hard to take in at first; everywhere you look commuting flocks of Great White Pelican, cormorants or Glossy Ibis will be flying in neat formations overhead, while Western Marsh Harriers quarter the reed beds at every turn and Eurasian Hobbies vie with Whiskered Terns (both very common here) to chase dragonflies. In the waterside bushes you soon come upon mixed colonies of Pygmy Cormorants, Little Egrets and various herons going about their breeding business, and the sharper-eyed may spot Penduline Tits at their remarkable hanging nests made from plant

Left: A quiet channel in the Danube Delta. Not surprisingly, this vast area can only effectively be explored by boat.

Below: A group of Great White Pelicans in their pink-tinged breeding plumage. More than 2,000 pairs breed in the delta.

down. Throughout each day you will be besieged by a constant chorus of reed bed birds such as Savi's, Moustached and Great Reed Warblers and Common Reed Bunting, heard together with the sharper notes of Common Moorhen and Water Rail. It is a good place to learn the art of listening.

A little more effort is needed to see some of the special species. One of these is the endangered Dalmatian Pelican, which still holds on in the delta but only in a few places, such as Lacul Sinoie in the south-east, where the main breeding island has recently been saved from destruction due to erosion; there are now probably fewer than 50 pairs in the delta. Other choice species include the White-tailed Eagle (about five breeding pairs) and the Red-footed Falcon (150 pairs), both of which range widely while hunting and should be seen, given a little time. Some of the more secretive marsh birds, such as Little and Spotted Crakes and Little Bittern, may also require patience to see, especially from a boat. Often the best strategy is to find some dry land and watch from there, where mud abuts the bottom of the reed stems.

Opposite: Small numbers of Rough-legged Buzzards spend the winter in the delta area.

Above: The globally threatened Lesser White-fronted Goose (note the distinctive yellow eye-ring) spends part of the early winter in the delta area, before shifting southwards.

Waders can be hard to find, although, as with everything on the delta, there are huge numbers here at times, mainly on passage. If you find a suitable area of shallow water, look out for three typical 'eastern' migrants: Temminck's Stint, Broad-billed Sandpiper and Marsh Sandpiper.

In winter the Danube Delta is just as impressive for numbers as it is in summer, although the birding is less comfortable. Nonetheless, winter counts of 500 Lesser White-fronted and 45,000 Red-breasted Geese (mainly in the southern part of the delta) should make most birders come running. Other counts that would be almost unimaginable in other parts of Europe include 32,000 Red-crested Pochards, 13,000 Ferruginous Ducks (also common in summer), 40,000 Northern Shovelers and 970,000 Common Pochards. All these birds, not surprisingly, attract raptors. The number of White-tailed Eagles may shoot up to 50; there will be a few Rough-legged Buzzards and even the odd Greater Spotted Eagle may show up.

The delta has recently gained some attention as a migration hot spot. Its convenient position on the Black Sea Flyway makes it well situated to receive

Below: One of the typical 'eastern' waders which passes through the delta on migration is the Marsh Sandpiper.

Opposite: Although the Danube Delta is better known for its breeding birds than for its migrants, the regular presence of birds such as Broad-billed Sandpiper show the huge potential of the area as a stopping-off point.

migrants from any points north or east. In the last few years Sahalin Island, at the mouth of the delta, has been acquiring a reputation as a good place for scarce birds such as Paddyfield Warbler and Red-throated Pipit.

On a discordant note, in the last couple of years the Danube Delta has suffered from a series of setbacks. In 2005 the delta was closed to visitors when bird flu was discovered nearby and not long afterwards devastating floods hit the area. Then, disastrously, the Ukrainian government sanctioned the construction of a ship canal through the northern part, potentially destroying some of the wildest and most bird-rich sections of the whole Biosphere Reserve. To the coldest hearts, it appears, not even the title of 'best place for birds in Europe' cuts very much ice.

CD tracks

TRACK 27: Great Reed Warbler
TRACK 28: Little Egret

Hortobágy

Site rank | 5

HABITAT | Grassland (puszta), lakes, marshes, fishponds, light agriculture, woodland

KEY SPECIES | Aquatic Warbler, Great Bustard, Saker Falcon, Common Crane, Pygmy Cormorant, Ferruginous Duck, Penduline Tit

TIME OF YEAR | All year

Many birders rank this site in the same class as such ornithological marvels as the Danube Delta and Coto Doñana. The superb mixture of habitats, which includes freshwater marshes, saline lakes, fishponds and the dry steppe habitat known as the puszta, all combine to produce an exceptional place for watching birds. A formidable 342 species have been recorded in the 800km^2 Hortobágy National Park, and in both spring and autumn it is perfectly possible to see 100 species in a day. Indeed, there is a regular bird race every year at the fishpond complex of Hortobágy-Halastó, where competitors are only allowed to travel on foot within a small complex with towers and hides. In September the winners tend to record 120–130 species in a single 24-hour period.

The Hortobágy lies within the Great Hungarian Plain to the south of the River Tisza, making this extremely flat country with wide open spaces and distant horizons (which partly explains how you can see a lot of species from a small area). Arguably, its most valuable habitat, and certainly its rarest, is the steppe, which is totally natural and once played host to prehistoric elephants and horses. The puszta mainly overlies alkaline soils, with an inconspicuous but very special flora (short-grass steppe) that is able to withstand the saline conditions; some parts have underlying loess soils, which are more productive (tall-grass steppe) and in the general region have often given way to small-scale cultivation. The most obvious inhabitants of the puszta are actually the local domestic animals: the Hungarian grey cattle, the Racka sheep with their spiral horns and the Mangalica pigs, all of which are rare breeds dating back two centuries or more.

Right: The domestic animals that graze the grasslands of the Hortobágy are of considerable interest, including these Hungarian Grey cattle.

Opposite: The stunning European Roller is common in the grasslands of the Hortobágy.

Right: Red-footed Falcons (this is a female) breed colonially in the small copses of trees that dot the plains.

The breeding birds here include Montagu's Harrier and Saker Falcon, the latter being more common in Hungary than pretty much everywhere else in Europe. Both feed on the small mammals that abound here, including hamsters. Another species, the Long-legged Buzzard, has recently started breeding here but is still rare.

Other birds of the short-grass country include the Eurasian Stone-curlew, Great Bustard (these can be hard to find) and two very different species that, nonetheless, practise the same perch-hunting technique: the European Roller and the Lesser Grey Shrike. Both are summer visitors to the invertebrate-rich plains here and both frequently perch on roadside wires to stake out large beetles, grasshoppers and small vertebrates, which they then dive on to from above. Both are common and the warmth of the ground under the summer sun keeps their prey numbers high.

The rich invertebrate fauna also suits another open-country bird, the Red-footed Falcon. This exciting, colourful species breeds in small colonies in isolated pockets of tall trees within the grassland, utilizing the old nests of other birds, usually members of the crow family. It can be seen throughout the area as it utilizes its various feeding techniques: hawking for insects in flight, hovering, perch-hunting and even walking on the ground. The adults feed themselves mainly on insects but they bring many softer, more nutritious items to the young, including frogs and toads, nestling birds and lizards. Intensely sociable, Red-footed Falcons often hunt together as well as breeding together, and just north of the Hortobágy, there is a large late-summer roost that may contain 1,000 birds.

The other main habitat in the Hortobágy, besides the puszta, is wetland, of which there are two main kinds: fishponds and marshes. Both are excellent for birds and contribute to the high list of species recorded in the area. Fishponds are particularly interesting because their active management dictates what is present; the water levels and water quality vary, as does their size, and all these factors mean that the birdlife varies too. So, for example, when a fishpond is drying out, the mud can contain thousands of waders in season (with Broad-billed Sandpiper a speciality), while at the same time various herons and storks (both White and Black Storks occur) wait on the margins for easy pickings. When a pond is full, however, it will be ideal for breeding and wintering wildfowl. On the various fishponds in the Hortobágy there are breeding Red-necked and Black-necked Grebes, Pygmy Cormorant, Ferruginous Duck, Little Crake, Whiskered Tern and White-winged Black Tern, each with its own distinct ecological requirements.

The various types of marshland within the Hortobágy, which extend out from the borders of the National Park to embrace the waters of the River Tisza, are superb for birds. The 127km^2 Lake Tisza, created by the damming of the river in the 1970s, is a maze of marshy backwaters, open water and water-lily-covered creeks

Below: Although actually easier to see in the agricultural centre of Hungary, the Saker Falcon is one of the Hortobágy's star birds.

and would be an exceptional site on its own, even without the vast network of reedy dykes, flooded puszta and marsh elsewhere in the neighbouring Hortobágy proper. Various herons abound in all these areas, including Squacco Heron and Little Bittern, while the riparian woods play host to Penduline Tit, and the reed beds and bushes throb to the songs of a variety of warblers, including Eurasian Reed, Great Reed, Savi's, Moustached, Marsh and River. In one or two spots, usually accessible only in the company of an official guide from the National Park, Aquatic Warblers breed. The small population of 400–600 singing males is the only one in Hungary.

An incidental quirk of the nearby River Tizsa is the famous annual mating of mayflies (*Palingenia longicauda*), which happens each year in the middle of June. For a couple of weeks, working downstream from Serbia and lasting for a day or two at each point along the Tizsa, it is possible to witness the waters of the river literally covered with millions of these insects, which are the largest mayflies in Europe (12cm from head to tail), as they dance over the surface in search of a mate. The mayfly 'flowering' only occurs in the right conditions of moon phase and temperature, for an hour or so in the evening. It is one of the continent's great wildlife events.

In the late autumn and early winter, the Hortobágy's proximity of wetland and open country attracts a whole new set of birds. It is, for example, the largest stopover site for Common Crane in the whole of Europe, playing host to some 80,000 birds at its peak in late October and November. The birds feed on the fields by day and come to the fishponds in the evening to roost, when they make a spectacular sight and sound.

Superb though the cranes are, they are not alone, because the general area is also a magnet for geese at the same time, including those species that prefer drier areas in which to feed – namely, Red-breasted and Lesser White-fronted Geese. Up to 50 of the latter may be seen, while there are only a handful of Red-breasted Geese, mainly in November. These rarities are found among larger flocks of Greater White-fronted and Greylag Geese and, like the Common Cranes, they all feed in surrounding fields and then retreat to the safety of wetlands, often fishponds, when it is time to go to roost. Few remain into December.

In the winter the Hortobágy is a harsh place, proven by the presence of flocks of such hardy birds as Snow and Lapland Buntings, Twite, Merlin and Rough-legged Buzzard. This is the time to see White-tailed Eagles. Although these huge birds are common in the area all year round, the winter population may number an incredible 80 individuals. At such a time it is possible to see several birds together, which makes yet another spectacular sight. Even in the depths of winter, this remarkable spot in Central Europe has plenty to enthral the birder.

CD tracks

TRACK 29: Little Crake
TRACK 30: Penduline Tit

Opposite: The Lesser Grey Shrike is one of the characteristic birds of the grasslands. It feeds on large insects, such as beetles, which abound here.

Below: Despite their size, Great Bustards are easily lost in the vast flat landscape, and can be extremely difficult to find.

100 Kalmykian Steppes

INFORMATION

SITE RANK | 21

HABITAT | Semi-desert, steppe, marshes, lakes

KEY SPECIES | Demoiselle Crane, Great and Little Bustards, Steppe Eagle, Ruddy Shelduck, Ménétries's Warbler, Rose-coloured Starling

TIME OF YEAR | Best in spring and early summer

Birders are renowned for being adventurous but, even so, not many make it out here, to the eastern fringe of Europe, where the culture and terrain lean towards Central Asia. Not even the lure of such superb birds as Demoiselle Crane, Blue-cheeked Bee-eater, Pallas's Gull and Rose-coloured Starling has managed to drag the birding community here in any numbers yet. But for those who do make it, the Kalmykian steppes offer opportunities not just for exciting birding but for discoveries too.

The Kalmyk Republic, as it is known, lies in that poorly known patch of land between the Black and the Caspian Seas. More precisely, it lies close to the western shore of the Caspian Sea, south and west of the River Volga. The people, the Kalmyks, are descended from nomadic herdsmen from the Kazakh–China border, who began to settle in the area in the 17th century. Intriguingly, they brought Buddhism with them, and today Kalmykia is the only state in Europe where Buddhism is the majority religion. The history of the people is, to say the least, turbulent. They have evacuated the area twice: first, intentionally in the mid-18th century, when things became sour with the Russians and 200,000 left in a single migration back towards their homeland; then, forcibly in December 1943, when Stalin accused the Kalmyks of siding with the German army and ordered the deportation of the entire people to Siberia and elsewhere. It is estimated that one-third of them died en route or shortly afterwards.

Furthermore, after they finally returned in 1957, the Kalmyks' homeland became subject to the usual disastrous Soviet environmental meddling. The fragile steppes that originally attracted them were ploughed or overgrazed and much of the area was transformed into semi-desert. However, it seems that both the people and the land are astonishingly resilient. Just recently it has been shown by satellite studies that large parts of the region, with their small human population, are now regenerating their original steppe vegetation – and that, of course, is good news for birders.

That doesn't make Kalmykia an easy place to watch wildlife. The whole area of so-called 'Pontic' steppe is about 100,000km^2 in extent; the birds move around and there aren't many stake-outs where species can be reliably seen. In summer, when the visitors, if there are any, come, it is stiflingly hot (40šC and above), with little relief over most of the area, which is extremely flat, some parts actually being a few metres below sea level. There are a number of Important Bird Areas, as defined by Birdlife International, and there is one state reserve, the Cherny

Opposite: The dry, open country of Kalmykia, between the Caspian and Black Seas, suits the rare Ménétries's Warbler.

Above: The stunning Blue-cheeked Bee-eater occurs along water-courses.

Zemly Zapovednik, which is actually composed of two widely dispersed areas, but, other than this, any birder is essentially on their own. Of course, this might change soon but, for now, every single visiting ornithologist is really a pioneer.

The stand-out bird of the Kalmykian feather-grass steppes is undoubtedly the stately Demoiselle Crane, for which this area, together with the Lower Volga, is the world headquarters. In contrast to Common Cranes (which occur here on passage), these reduced-size cranes, the smallest of their family in the world, are more dry-country residents than wetland birds, and they feed mainly on seeds in the breeding season, with good helpings of beetles and other invertebrates to add some protein. However, to succeed in breeding, they must have fresh water nearby that they can drink, so are usually found near streams. When the young are threatened by a predator, such as a Steppe Eagle, the parents sometimes lead the young to water, where they are perfectly capable of swimming. These birds depart very early from their breeding grounds, by August, and migrate at high levels, out of sight of people, to their wintering grounds in East Africa.

The semi-desert and steppe of the area is also highly suitable for bustards, which both breed here and occur on passage, the latter often in impressive

numbers. For example, in the region of Erdniyevskaya, more than 7,000 Little Bustards have been counted passing through in the autumn, and nearly 1,000 can be seen in the area south of Elista, the state capital. These birds often gather in flocks of hundreds, or sometimes thousands.

Among the many other steppe specialities of the region are Eurasian Stone-curlew, European Roller, Black-bellied Sandgrouse, Greater Short-toed and Calandra Larks (the main larks, although White-winged and Black Larks may occur in the winter), Isabelline Wheatear and Rose-coloured Starling, the latter often occurring in large flocks and breeding in rocky outcrops; these deliciously coloured birds feed

Right: Isabelline Wheatears are ground-dwelling birds with longer legs than most of their peers.

mainly on grasshoppers and locusts, which abound here, and can often be seen in flocks of hundreds, or even thousands. Where bushes grow there are other specialities, notably warblers, including (Eastern) Olivaceous and Booted Warblers and, a real highlight, the poorly known Ménétries's Warbler. The latter is similar to the widespread Sardinian Warbler but is a summer visitor adapted to the extreme dryness of the climate here. There are also several records of the Asian Desert Warbler in the Lower Volga and this species may occur here too.

Not surprisingly there are plenty of predators, not just of the birds but also of the very high small mammal population, which includes hamsters, voles and ground squirrels known as Sousliks. Several raptor species live hand in hand with these small herbivorous creatures and may prey almost exclusively upon them; they include the Eastern Imperial and Steppe Eagles, Long-legged Buzzard and Saker Falcon. The area, with its open landscape, is also a paradise for harriers, with all four European species, including the Pallid Harrier, present, although the Hen Harrier only occurs in the winter. Red-footed Falcon also occurs where there are suitable nest sites in trees.

Although the steppe is characterized by its dry climate, many of the specialized birds that occur in the area are associated with water: the many saline lakes that are dotted throughout the area. These lakes are often centres of activity for the birds throughout the year. One of the largest, the 344km^2 Manych-Gudilo Lake in the extreme north-west of Kalmykia, is partly protected within the Cherny Zemly Zapovednik. The birds that use these wetlands for breeding and wintering include such species as Black-necked Grebe, Eurasian Spoonbill, Ruddy Shelduck, Black-winged Pratincole, White-tailed Plover, Mediterranean and Pallas's Gulls, White-winged Black Tern and White-headed Duck. Another common species hereabouts is the Mute Swan, here not living as the semi-domesticated bird that is so familiar from town parks in Western Europe but in truly wild, migratory populations. The wetlands also attract such species as the gorgeous Blue-cheeked Bee-eater, here found alongside the much commoner European Bee-eater.

No birder is likely to encounter all of the species mentioned above but what they might just do is discover something else. At the moment the Cherny Zemly reserve receives annual visitor numbers of about 50 a year, most of whom come from within Russia itself and are not necessarily birders. What might happen if you turned up and did some bird counts? It would be horrendously hot; it would be primitive; there wouldn't be much comfort – but pioneers were never ones to settle for an easy life.

Below: The striking Pallas's Gull winters on the steppes. It breeds on nearby islands in the Caspian Sea.

Pripyat River

SITE RANK | 3

HABITAT | Meandering river with oxbow lakes, meadows, fens, reed swamp, forest, bogs

KEY SPECIES | Azure Tit, Terek Sandpiper, Great Snipe, Aquatic Warbler, Greater Spotted Eagle, Corncrake, Spotted Crake, Little Crake, Eurasian Three-toed Woodpecker, White-backed Woodpecker, Thrush Nightingale

TIME OF YEAR | Spring is best but undoubtedly interesting all year

The Pripyat River, in the south of Belarus, has been dubbed the 'Amazon of Europe', and while such a comparison is a bit far-fetched for a river only 710km long, there is no doubt that, in European terms, it is without parallel for the sheer area of bird-rich, largely intact habitat that still remains there. Wilderness is an overused term for most places but not here. For more than 250km of its journey between the hills of northern Ukraine and the Dnieper, the Pripyat winds unmolested, creating a truly vast network of bogs, mires, flood meadows, riverine woodland and forest, much of which is rarely, if ever, visited by people. With a list of more than 200 breeding bird species, many of them extremely rare or dangerously declining in the rest of Europe, this area – while barely known to most western birders – could yet prove, in terms of diversity and the number of rarities, to be Europe's premier wetland.

The sheer size of the Pripyat wilderness is what makes it, in a European context, so important and unique. Take the Pripyatski National Park, for instance. This maze of oak, pine and alder forest, dotted with bogs and other wetlands, is no less than 825km^2 in size, yet forms only a part of the overall site. The mid-Pripyat Important Bird Area (as designated by Birdlife International) covers an additional 904km^2, following 120km of the river's meanders (between 4 and 14km wide). And there are several smaller additional sites that would be major birding areas if they had not been concealed inside this previously poorly known birding country for such a long time. While definitely not easy to cover, there is no doubt that what a visitor will encounter here is stuff that dreams are made of further west.

A small but representative locality along the Pripyat River is Turov Meadow, opposite the village of the same name, which, incidentally, makes a good centre for exploration. This site boasts an ornithological station which has been used for ringing studies since 1996. The main subjects are waders, which use the site in hordes in spring and autumn, with very healthy numbers staying to breed. Twenty-four wader species have been caught here, of which the most numerous are Ruffs; between 20,000 and 25,000 pass through every spring and the meadow is perhaps one of the best and easiest sites anywhere to witness the multicoloured males displaying communally at their 'leks'. Together with enormous numbers of Common Redshank, Whiskered and White-winged Black Terns and Little Gull, the meadows simply teem with birds. Amidst the hordes are several rarities, notably the Terek Sandpiper, here at something of an outpost in terms of its distribution (most are in Russia), and the Great Snipe, of which there

are 30–50 displaying males. The Terek Sandpiper prefers to nest close to rivers, where it can gain access to the silted, muddy banks. There are perhaps fewer than 100 pairs in Belarus.

The Turov area is more than just a meadow, however. In the village itself, and nearby within thickets of willow along the meanders, it is possible to find one of Europe's most sought-after passerines, the exquisite Azure Tit. This stunning bird, which looks like a delicately frosted version of the Blue Tit, is a temperate Asian species that is very uncommon west of the Volga; Belarus is the easiest place to find it in Europe. A sighting needs to be worked for, however, because this is a remarkably elusive bird, given to spending long periods of time concealed within the thick riparian vegetation.

To the west of Turov is the mid-Pripyat IBA mentioned above, the meander between the Yaselda and Stviga tributaries, where fairly recent surveys have revealed no less than 155 breeding species, in numbers to make western ornithologists blush. For example, there are 2,000 singing Corncrake males,

Above: The small population of Terek Sandpipers in Belarus forms an outpost away from the main breeding areas farther north. The birds breed along muddy banks.

700 Spotted Crake and 300 Little Crake, along with enormous numbers of herons, warblers, ducks, terns and waders, including, just as examples, 10,000 pairs of Garganey, 150 pairs of Ferruginous Duck, 70 pairs of Black Stork and 7,000 pairs of White-winged Black Tern. And these are some of the more widespread birds. Among the jewels in the crown are the 1,000 displaying male Great Snipe, up to 20 pairs of Greater Spotted Eagle and 400 singing male Aquatic Warblers.

To the east, between the Stviga confluence and the Ubort river (the name 'Pripyat' refers to the five tributaries), lies Pripyatski National Park. Two hundred and forty-six species have been recorded here, of which nearly 200 breed, and once again these include some great rarities of high conservation concern, including Greater Spotted Eagle (4–6 pairs) and Great Snipe (up to 150 males). But perhaps here it is the diversity that is key, both in the habitat and in the birdlife. There are wooded and open peat bogs, forests of alder, pine and ancient oak, seasonally inundated grassland, canals, marshes, lakes and pools, and some cultivation. Among the many highlights are Azure Tit, Aquatic Warbler, Terek Sandpiper, eight species of woodpecker (including Eurasian Three-toed and White-backed), Lesser Spotted Eagle, Pallid Harrier, and Collared and Red-breasted Flycatchers.

Opposite: Arguably the Pripyat's star avian attraction is the sparkling Azure Tit, which is an elusive bird of riverside tangles.

Above: The enormous wetlands along the river host huge numbers of rails and crakes, including the Little Crake.

Above: More than just a wetland, the forest areas along the river hold all of Europe's woodpecker species, including the Eurasian Three-toed. The yellow crown identifies this bird as a male.

CD tracks

TRACK 33: Black-tailed Godwit
TRACK 34: Azure Tit

While these sites are the largest preserved areas, there are other places within the Pripyat drainage that host similar mind-boggling numbers of birds. The enormous bog, fen (mire) and forest complex of Olmany, for example, still used as a military training area, may hold as many as 30 pairs of Greater Spotted Eagle and 20 displaying Great Snipe, along with, for example, 40 pairs of Common Crane and 20 pairs of Black Stork, while the supporting cast includes the largest population of Great Grey Owl in the country. At Lelchitsky-Ubort, to the south-east of Pripyatsky, is a 750ha bog with another 100 singing male Aquatic Warblers, a significant proportion of the world population of this bird, yet simply swamped by the higher number elsewhere in the area.

The story of the Aquatic Warblers is intriguing. Although it had been known for many years that this rare species bred in Belarus, nobody had any idea how many until comparatively recently. With the species in such sharp decline almost everywhere, and with it having become extinct in France, Belgium, Italy and the Netherlands during the 20th century, ornithologists were despatched to this poorly known area in 1995 to find out. What they came back with stunned conservationists; the small warbler was flourishing in hitherto unforeseen numbers. Amazingly, no less than two-thirds of the known population (maximum 14,200 singing males) has been discovered since 1995.

The current relatively happy state of the Pripyat area – as a wonderland becoming increasingly better known by birders – is quite a contrast to the area's sombre infamy conferred upon it 25 years ago. For it was only a short distance from here, in neighbouring Ukraine, that the Chernobyl nuclear disaster occurred on 26 April 1986. The city of Pripyat, on the river downstream from the best birding areas, was evacuated a day later and even today remains a ghost town, being totally uninhabited and within the 30km exclusion zone around the stricken plant. Had the nuclear plant been further west, who knows what might have happened to the magical area described in this section. Its claim to be the 'Amazon of Europe' would have been even less appropriate.

Below: Grassland areas hold open country species such as the Pallid Harrier.

Bialowieza Forest

INFORMATION

SITE RANK | 15

HABITAT | Old-growth and managed forest; meadow

KEY SPECIES | Woodpeckers including White-backed and Eurasian Three-toed, flycatchers including Collared and Red-breasted, raptors, Thrush Nightingale, River Warbler, Corncrake

TIME OF YEAR | Best in spring and early summer, particularly May and June, but interesting all year round

Despite the vast number of forests of all kinds that are found in Europe, cropping up in every corner of the continent, there is a surprising level of agreement among ornithologists about which is the best one of all for birds. Such is the sparkling reputation of Bialowieza, and such is the universal delight of those who have visited it at what they have seen, that this vast lowland stretch on the border between Poland and Belarus would appear to be head and shoulders above the competition.

In many ways the Puszcaz Bialowieza, or as it is known in Belarus the Belavezhskaya Pushcha, is unique, being the largest remaining, relatively intact area of lowland deciduous/mixed forest in Europe. It measures some 50km from north to south and west to east and is a remnant of the wild wood that once covered vast areas of the European Plain. Some parts have been untouched for more than a century, allowing the trees to grow to enormous heights (some over 50m) and enabling the natural process of forest succession to run its course, with dead and decaying wood left in place. Not surprisingly, species diversity is extremely high and includes nearly 170 species of breeding bird, 55 species of mammal, 900 species of vascular plant, 1,500 species of fungi and many thousands of invertebrates.

This is definitely not an area in which to rush about looking for birds; it is best to stand still and let the inhabitants show themselves one by one. Besides, the very special atmosphere in the strictly protected areas in spring and summer, standing in the dappled shade of the multi-layered forest and dwarfed by the towering trees, tends to instil hush in even the most fevered birder. Europeans are no longer accustomed to this kind of place, despite centuries of love–hate folklore about vast, mysterious forests.

Even a person with little knowledge of birds would expect woods to attract woodpeckers, and Bialowieza boasts a proud list of nine species. One of these, the White-backed Woodpecker, is a major beneficiary of the park's protected status, since it cannot sustain itself whenever forests are over-managed and no significant rotting timber is available. Moreover, the dominant woodland community of Bialowieza, which is made up of mixed stands of oak, lime and hornbeam, also suits the pernickety Middle Spotted Woodpecker, an oak specialist. The mighty Black Woodpecker and the Grey-headed Woodpecker could almost be described as common, and in the park's spruce forests the Eurasian Three-toed Woodpecker can also be found, although it tends to be quiet and elusive.

The presence of Eurasian Three-toed Woodpecker, together with such other northern species as Tengmalm's Owl, Eurasian Pygmy Owl and Spotted Nutcracker, reflects the park's position at the transition zone between European coniferous and European deciduous forest. Norway Spruce reaches its southern limit here and Sessile Oak is at its north-eastern extremity. This mixing allows for some 12 different forest communities to flourish in the park. The oak, lime and hornbeam forest is the most widespread but other important communities include pine, spruce and oak and, in the wetter areas, alder and pine.

The deciduous sector is excellent for flycatchers, with four species breeding. The Spotted Flycatcher is common; the European Pied Flycatcher benefits from the presence of Sessile Oak, while the Collared Flycatcher and the Red-breasted Flycatcher are seen here as reliably as anywhere in Europe. All breed in natural holes in the mighty trees and all might need considerable patience to see. The Red-breasted Flycatcher is an especially difficult species to locate, because it is a canopy feeder that shuns the open perches favoured by the others.

Below: A European Bison in winter. Without the presence of these rare herbivores at Bialowieza, the forest would probably not have been preserved as it has.

Other common smaller birds of the deciduous areas include Wood Warbler, Hawfinch, Willow and Crested Tits and Eurasian Golden Oriole. The Greenish Warbler is also found in the old-growth woodland and shares with the Red-breasted Flycatcher the quirk of migrating to Asia, rather than Africa, for the winter.

Aside from the forest itself, the reserve contains significant clearings and marshland areas on both sides of the border. Unsurprisingly, these sites hold a different suite of species from the forest proper. A walk in such an area is likely to reveal Thrush Nightingale, Common Rosefinch, Red-backed Shrike and Barred and River Warblers, while two rare and declining species also occur: the Corncrake, which is still relatively numerous, and the Great Snipe, which occurs only sparingly. Black Storks rely on the juxtaposition of marsh and forest, feeding in the former and breeding in the latter, while Lesser Spotted Eagles are somewhat similar, requiring forest for breeding and open country over which they can forage.

As well as the Lesser Spotted Eagle, the area generally is excellent for raptors and about 15 species breed here. As might be expected for a large, forested area, the wasp-eating European Honey-buzzard is numerous, although, as ever, highly elusive when breeding. Montagu's Harrier occurs on the open areas and the Short-

Opposite: The White-backed Woodpecker cannot cope with forestry practices such as the removal of dead trees. It thrives in the undisturbed woodlands.

Above: Lesser Spotted Eagles require the juxtaposition of forest for breeding and open country for hunting.

CD tracks

TRACK 35: White-backed Woodpecker
TRACK 36: Red-breasted Flycatcher

toed Eagle can be seen soaring in search of the park's various species of snake. The Booted Eagle is another large raptor breeding here, feeding mainly on birds, which it captures with spectacular plunges from a great height.

Birders will need to choose which kinds of forest to go birding in. On the Polish side there is a strictly protected zone of about 50km^2, in which there is no management whatsoever and entry is strictly by permit along a single 4km route. There is also a much broader, managed zone, where visitors can walk relatively freely. The core zone is much more exciting and atmospheric, while the managed area outside is actually somewhat easier to work for birds. On the Belarusian side the park has three zones: a core area (157km^2), a buffer zone and a transition zone, the latter allowing some farming and other commercial practices. Within its larger core zone, the Belarusian park authorities have several designated oaks of more than 400–600 years old, together with ashes and pines over 350 years old and spruces up to 250 years old. It is these that add to the magic of the whole place, quite apart from its variety of birds and other wildlife.

Incidentally, birders have a special park inhabitant to thank for the continued existence of Bialowieza: the European Bison, or Wisent. It was the presence of this huge mammal that originally marked the area out as special and Bialowieza has spent much of its history as a hunting reserve for the rich and influential. A visit to the area would not be complete without at least one sighting of this four-legged icon.

Right: Collared Flycatchers are one of four species of flycatcher that flourish at Bialowieza. Seeing all four in a day requires a certain degree of luck and persistence.

Opposite: Easy to hear but difficult to see, the River Warbler is a retiring species of dense, damp shrubbery.

Biebrza River

Ornithologically, north-east Poland is well and truly spoilt. Not only does it boast Europe's largest primeval forest (Bialowieza, see page 112) but the site described here, Biebrza Marshes, has a strong claim to be one of the finest wetlands on the continent – and it's only 100km or so away from Bialowieza. No wonder that Poland is currently one of the most popular destinations in Europe for visiting birders.

The vast marshes here run for more than 100km along the sluggish, meandering Biebrza River, roughly between the towns of Augustów and Lomza, within the cold and damp Podlaskie province. The wetlands are not all one unit but are ecologically diverse, encompassing some 70 different micro-habitats, each defined by their vegetation mix. This is one key to the site's importance. With 181 species of birds recorded breeding within Bierbrza National Park to date and 270 species noted in all, very few places on the continent can match this area in terms of avian diversity.

The marshland's other key benefit lies in the relatively pristine state of its lifeblood and source, the Biebrza River. This waterway rises in the moraine hills close to Sokólka, on the border with Belarus, and it flows west for a mere 164km before emptying into the River Narew close to Lomza. For a wide variety of reasons, including, no doubt, its proximity to the border area with the former Soviet Union, this short stretch has hardly been tampered with at all by people, making it almost unique among lowland rivers in Europe. As a result, many of the habitats are completely natural and at their very best for biodiversity. Sadly, they showcase what we in Europe have lost.

The Biebrza valley can conveniently be divided into three sections. The upper basin consists of the narrow river passing through peaty deposits, with bogs, meadows and some mixed forest. The middle basin is rich in fen vegetation, including sedge beds and meadows. The lower basin floods in spring and also boasts fens, reed beds and more forest. Where areas are seasonally inundated, sedge beds flourish, which play host to some of the site's rarest birds, including Aquatic Warbler. Meanwhile, flood meadows are ideal for such breeding birds as Ruff.

One of the species that originally caught the imagination of birders from Western Europe when Poland began to open up in the 1980s was the Great Snipe. Once widespread in lowland Europe, it had declined to near-extinction almost everywhere south of Scandinavia. But here in north-east Poland it held on in some

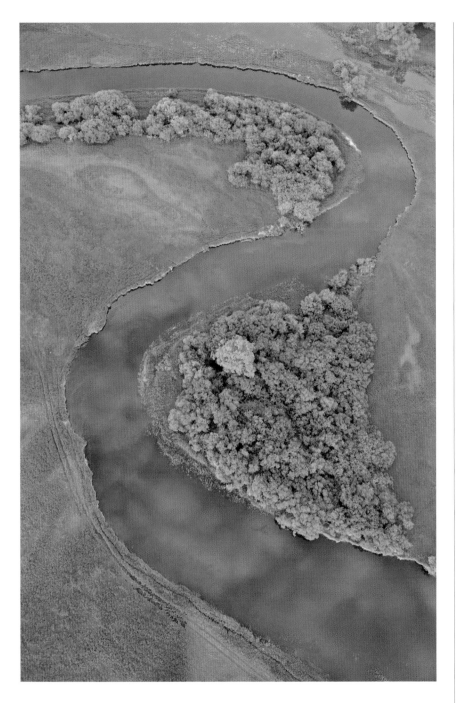

Left: The gentle meanders of an undisturbed river. The Biebrza runs for 100km through relatively pristine habitat.

numbers (there are 400–500 displaying males in the valley) and, even more importantly, it was actually possible to see this highly secretive species. A far-sighted local birder, Marek Borkowski, bought up the land containing the largest Great Snipe gathering ground (lek) and made a platform so that the birds were visible when they displayed at dusk. Today his private nature reserve, at Budy near the small village of Dobarz, still welcomes birders to enjoy the unusual sight and sound of the Great Snipe lek. It is quite a performance. Small numbers of males gather on the ground, ruffle their feathers, puff out their chests and make entertaining 'flutter-jumps' while uttering a quite extraordinary song consisting of a twittering, a clicking like the sound of a bouncing table tennis ball coming to rest and, finally, a strange whining. The antics of the birds on the ground have been compared to children jumping on a bouncy castle.

Birders who come for the Great Snipe lek always have the chance of an almost unique quadruple. A small number of Jack Snipe also breed in Biebrza, way south of their usual boreal range and these, along with Common Snipe and Eurasian Woodcock, can sometimes be seen in the same evening.

Another of the highlights of the Biebrza River valley is the presence of the rare Aquatic Warbler, which only breeds in partly inundated sedge beds. There are between 2,000 and 3,000 singing males of this highly polygamous warbler in the area, and the National Park is dotted with special places where they can be seen,

Left: Birders fed up with difficult-to-see species can always enjoy the numerous White Storks.

notably near Gugny, which is a special reserve set up for their study. Although Aquatic Warblers prefer to sing at dusk, they have a habit of starting a performance low in the vegetation and gradually working their way into view, so most visitors manage to see them well.

Besides these great rarities, there are obviously a great many other species to see in the Biebrza River area. Or at least you can try to see them. Besides the tricky Great Snipe and Aquatic Warbler, another increasingly uncommon species Europe-wide that abounds here but tends to sing at dusk and at night is the Corncrake. There are at least 2,000 singing males in the river basin and they make loud enough grating sounds to keep you awake at night but that does not mean that any birder will get a sniff at seeing them. Indeed, the same applies to the Spotted Crake, with its whiplash-like advertising call (up to 1,500 pairs), and the Little Crake, with its yapping call (up to 80 pairs). Add in Grasshopper and River Warblers (both common) and the equally publicity-shy Thrush Nightingale and you have an impressive suite of noisy but difficult-to-see species.

Birders hoping for light relief can always rely on the Biebrza's far showier wader population. Ruffs are common on the many meadows, with each male sporting its own colours, while Black-tailed Godwits, bedecked in colourful orange, are hard to miss. Or visitors can enjoy the area's terns, which include the complete trio of the dark-plumaged, insectivorous 'marsh terns' – Whiskered Tern, Black Tern and White-winged Black Tern – each of which nests on floating vegetation, particularly water lily pads. The last-named species tends to breed in more transitional, shallower habitats than the other two, such as newly flooded fields, and so its numbers each year depend on the prevailing water levels. Another set of birds that are easy to see are the long-legged wading birds, which include Common Crane and both European species of stork.

The whole area, with its patchwork of open areas and forested country, is also excellent for birds of prey. The biggest prize is the Greater Spotted Eagle, which is

Right: One of the most famous breeding birds of Bierbrza is the globally threatened Great Snipe. Males gather to display in small leks, in which they jump about and make strange buzzing noises.

Above: All three marsh terns breed in the wetlands, often choosing water-lily pads on which to place their nests. This is a White-winged Black Tern.

mainly found in the middle basin, although it is extremely difficult to see even there and also hard to identify from the very similar and much more numerous Lesser Spotted Eagle. Both these eagles eat similar prey but the Greater Spotted tends to take larger items and is more of a wetland species. Both share the skies with a healthy population of White-tailed Eagle and there are a few Golden and Short-toed Eagles too. Among the other raptors are large numbers of Western Marsh, Hen and Montagu's Harriers.

The forests are less celebrated than the superb wetlands of the Biebrza valley but they shouldn't be ignored. There are several leks of Black Grouse in the area, which can readily be visited in the spring, and other woodland specialities range from White-backed Woodpecker to Red-breasted Flycatcher.

Despite its obvious riches, it should be added that Biebrza is very much a spring and summer site. As mentioned above, the area is a bit cold and grim in the autumn and winter, with, on average, 140 days of snow cover a year in the upper basin and 117 days per year of sub-zero temperatures. These conditions plus 70 mornings a year with fog cover, as the waters of the Biebrza River touch the cold air sinking from the surrounding hills, and you can conclude that the area is best left alone until it get warmer. In the winter, birders can sit back and plan their visits.

CD tracks

TRACK 37: Great Snipe
TRACK 38: Thrush Nightingale

124 # High Tatras

INFORMATION

SITE RANK | 29

HABITAT | Forest and mountain

KEY SPECIES | Black, Syrian, White-backed, Grey-headed and Eurasian Three-toed Woodpeckers, Tengmalm's, Eurasian Pygmy and Eurasian Eagle Owls, Spotted Nutcracker, Western Capercaillie, Alpine Accentor, Wallcreeper

TIME OF YEAR | Best in spring and early summer, particularly from April to July

This national park in the heart of Europe is a delicious mixture of the convenient and the untamed. In these mountains are healthy populations of large mammals, such as Lynx and Brown Bear, creatures that need wild and quiet corners in which to live, far away from people. There is also a superb range of mountain and forest birds, many of them rare and equally retiring. Yet, despite its wild inhabitants' need for space, it is a convenient area to work; the Slovak part of the mountain range is comparatively compact, at only 741km^2, and the area attracts large numbers of tourists for walking in summer and skiing in winter, so there is plenty of accommodation nearby. As a bonus, there are 600km of well-marked trails, reaching ten of the high peaks. For a bit of luxury, there are even cable cars to take visitors into the alpine zone (above 1,800m).

Nevertheless, in the forests of the lower slopes it is easy to imagine that you are far from civilization. Early in the season, in April for example, it is possible to walk for many hours without coming across another human visitor; take care, however, because the weather can easily turn a gentle hike into a fight for survival. In this comparative wilderness such birds as the Western Capercaillie thrive. Europe's largest grouse is a shy species but there are estimated to be over 100 male birds in the national park (and many more females), and if you are very fortunate you may come across a small group of birds in display, strutting on the ground and making petulant jumps into the air, to a background of loud belches and odd popping noises, like the release of champagne corks. Extraordinarily, these birds often feed on nothing more than conifer needles for the whole of the winter. The Hazel Grouse is another species of the deep forest, detected by its extraordinarily high-pitched whistling song, while the Black Grouse is often seen at the edge of clearings. Both these species are perhaps easiest to see in the autumn, when both feed on the rich crop of fruiting trees and shrubs.

The very richness of these forests is illustrated by the fact that, within this relatively small area, no fewer than ten species of woodpecker occur, each with its own specific ecological requirements and favourite trees. One of the star birds of the High Tatras, for example, is the Eurasian Three-toed Woodpecker. Scarce over much of Europe, this species is locally common here, occurring in the older stands of spruce where dead wood is left to rot; it specializes in searching for the larvae and pupae of wood-boring beetles. The White-backed Woodpecker has a similar diet but is drawn to deciduous forests rather than conifers. It is scarce but can be found in stands of beech or aspen, its presence betrayed by deep gashes at the base of dead or rotting trees. Meanwhile, the local oak woods are favoured by the Middle Spotted Woodpecker, which gleans most of its food from the surface of the bark. Lesser Spotted Woodpeckers exist in stands of alder and other deciduous trees, while Black Woodpeckers favour mixed beech forest and Great Spotted Woodpeckers tend to occur in the conifers at higher altitudes. Grey-headed

Below: It might be small in stature, but the Starling-sized Eurasian Pygmy Owl is a formidable predator of small birds.

Woodpeckers are an indicator of mature deciduous woodland, and the picture is completed by the Syrian Woodpecker, the European Green Woodpecker and the unusual Eurasian Wryneck, species favouring more open areas at low altitude. Both the last-named species are ant specialists, seeking out colonies of these insects on the ground or on the lower branches of trees.

It seems to be a feature in Europe that where there are woodpecker species in quantity there are often owls too, which are also forest dwellers that can be fussy about their habitat requirements. In the High Tatras there is a good suite of species of the latter, several of which are much commoner farther north, in the Scandinavian taiga, and whose Carpathian populations are isolated outposts. Eurasian Pygmy and Tengmalm's Owls inhabit spruce and spruce/pine forests hereabouts, mainly above 900m, while the Eurasian Eagle Owl nests on rugged cliffs and gorges. There are a few Ural Owls in the beech forests in the eastern part of the national park, in the Belianske Tatra, but they are hard to find, being somewhat quieter and more retiring than many other owl species.

Below: A Ural Owl beautifully camouflaged against a forest tree. In the Tatras these birds are mainly found in beech forest.

This steep mountain range is a good place for the hiker to observe changes in habitat and bird life as the altitude increases. For example, on the lowest ground within the national park Corncrakes breed in the meadows, and the woods support species such as Red-breasted Flycatcher, Firecrest and Lesser Spotted Eagle. Above 900m the montane zone begins; here the woodland is mainly coniferous and birds such as Western Capercaillie and Crested Tit are commoner than lower down. In the sub-montane zone, at 1,200m, some Arolla pine grows and provides a niche for the Spotted Nutcracker. At 1,500m the tree cover begins to be dominated by mountain pine, with dwarf shrubs growing underneath (the subalpine zone), where species such as Common Redpoll and Ring Ouzel eke out a living. Finally, above 1,850m, the trees give way to a rugged, boulder-strewn alpine tundra.

There are not many species on these very high tops but those present are charismatic and intriguing. The main predator up here is the Golden Eagle, which is relatively easy to see and quite unfazed by the often violent changes in the weather that commonly afflict these mountains, even in summer – visitors beware. Water Pipits breed in good numbers, favouring areas with short grass, and Rufous-tailed Rock Thrushes breed among the boulders. On scree slopes there are

Top: The peaks of the High Tatras reach 2,655m in altitude, with 11 peaks over 2,500m.

Above: The Hazel Grouse is one of three species of grouse found within the national park. They are all tricky to see.

Alpine Accentors, which have recently been discovered to have an extraordinary mating system. A group of three to six males and three to five females live together and any given individual may copulate with all the members of the opposite sex, while trying to prevent the others from doing the same. To attempt to safeguard their paternity, male Alpine Accentors may mate more than 100 times a day.

One further species occurring at these high levels is the Wallcreeper, an extraordinary passerine with a long, curved bill and broad, butterfly-like wings of brilliant crimson, dotted with black and white. It feeds on invertebrates gleaned from tall rock faces or gathered by the sides of streams, and when moving up and down a rock face has a habit of constantly opening its wings to reveal the bright colours. The Wallcreeper is harder to find here than in some other mountain locations in Europe. But where, other than in these wild, unspoilt mountains, could there be a better setting for such a bird?

CD tracks

TRACK 39: Western Capercaillie
TRACK 40: Black Woodpecker

Opposite: Spotted Nutcrackers are associated with the Arolla Pine, and are found mainly between 1,200m and 1,400m.

Below: The stunning Rufous-tailed Rock Thrush breeds among boulders in the alpine zone.

Wadden Sea

INFORMATION

SITE RANK | 11

HABITAT | A long stretch of coast, including intertidal mudflats, salt marsh, dunes, barrier islands, freshwater marshes, grazing meadows and scrub

KEY SPECIES | Huge numbers of wildfowl and waders, including Common Shelduck and Pied Avocet, gulls, terns including Gull-billed, raptors

TIME OF YEAR | All year round

It seems hard to believe that three of Europe's most densely populated and industrialized countries could contain within their borders anything that could be described as 'wilderness'. And yet, incredibly, stretching along the North Sea coast from Den Helde in the Netherlands to the busy port of Esbjerg in Denmark is the Wadden Sea, 9,000km^2 of lonely, windswept, wild coastline where the footsteps of people cannot be seen and where people have not yet come to abuse and destroy the environment. No human can live here on the roughly 10km-wide skirt of perilous intertidal mudflats and salt marshes that rims this 500km stretch of coast and, miraculously, the greedy hands of developers have been largely kept at bay.

The Wadden Sea is of crucial importance to Europe's birds. In the German section alone, it is thought that some 1.5 million wildfowl and up to 4 million waders, gulls and terns use the rich feeding grounds for at least some of the year, and if it were not for the food-rich, sheltered and safe waters of the Wadden Sea, they would be dispersed and depleted to an extent that is hard to imagine. Almost all the Common Shelduck in Western Europe congregate on the Wadden Sea between July and September in order to moult. Hundreds of thousands of waders use the estuarine ooze for refuelling on migration flights or for sustaining themselves during the winter months. Without the Wadden Sea they would struggle to find the resources they need.

The sheer numbers of birds using the site are staggering. Counts of waders using the German section as a staging area on their migration include 463,000 Eurasian Oystercatchers, 400,000 Red Knots, 628,000 Dunlin, 192,000 Bar-tailed Godwits and 97,000 Eurasian Curlews. The Schleswig–Holstein Wadden Sea National Park, just one section of this, holds winter populations of 26,000 Barnacle Geese and 150,000 Common Eiders, while 133,000 Brent Geese, 104,000 Northern Pintails, 19,000 Curlew Sandpipers and 15,000 Sandwich Terns pass through on migration. In the Danish section, the Vadehavet area sees 35,000 Common Scoters, 10,000 Pink-footed Geese, 43,600 European Golden Plovers and 365,000 Dunlin pass by, while in the Netherlands a highly impressive total of 15,000 Pied Avocets has been counted on passage, along with 29,000 Grey Plovers. Not surprisingly, since the Wadden Sea is a huge site and the birds are constantly moving, it is difficult, if not impossible, to get complete counts for the whole area. However, for Common Shelduck the situation is slightly different because most of them congregate in the Schleswig–Holstein National Park. Here 150,000 of these

bold black, white, bottle-green and chestnut ducks while away the late summer, feeding in these rich, shallow waters whilst they exchange old flight feathers for new ones. Interestingly, this gathering does not include the youngsters, who remain in the breeding areas, initially under the care of a small number of selected adults.

Birding the Wadden Sea is, not surprisingly, very rewarding, and not just for big numbers. Right across from the Netherlands to Denmark there are superb

Above: The vast mudflats of the Wadden Sea provide food and refuge for masses of migrating waders – these are Bar-tailed Godwits.

locations, hosting an excellent variety of species throughout the year. In Denmark, for example, at the very northern tip of the Wadden Sea, the sandy peninsula of Skallingen is the location for one of Denmark's most famous bird observatories, Blåvandshuk. A superb migration watch point, it attracts ducks, geese and waders, like much of the rest of the area, but also, at times, seabirds, including skuas and even storm-petrels. Further south, a group of barrier islands lie along the coast right down to the German border, including several that are excellent for birds. Romo, like many of the sites on the Wadden Sea, has freshwater marshes as well as saline habitats, and here birds such as Red-necked Grebe, Eurasian Bittern, Spotted Crake and Bearded and Penduline Tits breed. In the marshes, heathland and dunes a trio of harriers – Hen, Montagu's and Western Marsh – all breed and gorge themselves on the plenty. In winter, Rough-legged Buzzards and even White-tailed Eagles patrol the general area.

Another good barrier island is Fano, to the north. About 20,000 ducks, geese and waders use this 16km-long island as a staging post on migration. In addition, it hosts a number of species that are especially attracted to the peculiar nature of the Wadden Sea and are thus widespread throughout the area. These include the Kentish Plover, which is drawn to flat, sandy beaches, and the Pied Avocet, which

Opposite: Barnacle Geese taking a rest on the Wadden Sea. The importance of this site lies not only in its wintering and breeding birds, but also for birds that spend short periods in transit.

Above: Most of the Common Shelducks of Western Europe travel to the German part of the Wadden Sea in order to moult. They arrive in July and leave from October onwards.

relishes the shallow, saline water. Throughout the Wadden Sea, low shingle and beaches provide excellent breeding habitat for terns, including Common, Arctic, Sandwich, Little and Gull-billed. Fano is also a noted area for visible migration, not just for waterbirds but also for passerines such as pipits and finches.

At the other end of the Wadden Sea, in the Netherlands, there is another set of barrier islands, offering similar habitats to those in Denmark and Germany. The most famous of these is Texel, which holds a superb variety of breeding birds, including Eurasian Spoonbill and Black-tailed Godwit, and even provides a little woodland for such species as Short-toed Treecreeper, Hawfinch and Long-eared Owl. It is a superb place for observing migration, including passerines. Visitors include 'regular' rarities such as Yellow-browed and Pallas's Leaf Warblers.

However, Texel is far removed from the core part of the Wadden Sea. In truth, the value in this remarkable area is in its lonely flats, beaches and dunes, where the birds can feed for days, or even months at a time, without being seen or disturbed by a single human being.

CD tracks

TRACK 41: Spotted Crake
TRACK 42: Sandwich Tern

Opposite: Many of the islands of the Wadden Sea have freshwater marshes, where birds such as the Eurasian Bittern breed.

Below: Penduline Tits also occur in freshwater marshes, using the 'wool' from bulrushes and willows to build their nests in the surrounding bushes.

North Norfolk

INFORMATION

SITE RANK | 14

HABITAT | Coast, mudflats, salt marsh, dunes, freshwater pools and marshes, shingle, scrub and woodland

KEY SPECIES | [Dark-bellied] Brent and Pink-footed Geese, Red Knot, Dunlin, Pied Avocet, Barn Owl, Bearded Tit, Shore Lark, Twite

TIME OF YEAR | All year, although mid-summer (June and July) can be quiet apart from the breeding birds

Opposite: Sandwich Terns, which are notoriously fickle about their breeding sites, nest regularly on Scolt Head Island and Blakeney Point.

While London might be the hub of Britain as far as most tourists are concerned, for the visiting birder there is only one place to go to catch up with the ornithological scene and that is North Norfolk. This somewhat featureless corner of the east of England has an extraordinarily rich history for both birds and birdwatching. Its position close to the Continent and at the southern shore of the chilly North Sea makes it a magnet for all kinds of avian arrivals, while the presence of a virtual colony of top birders, attracted by the eccentricities of the avifauna, has made it one of the liveliest ornithologists' hot spots in Europe. It's a place where every cluster of binocular-clad people could be made up of everything from complete beginners to fully fledged professionals, of many nationalities. To illustrate the magic of the place, the tiny reserve of Titchwell Marsh receives some 120,000 human visitors a year, making it one of the most popular reserves in the entire world.

North Norfolk certainly has plenty to attract birders, with delights all year round. It hosts some scarce breeding birds and impressive numbers of waders and wildfowl in winter, while the two main migration seasons, April to May and August to November, bring an almost bewildering variety of birds. More than 360 species have been recorded between the estuary of The Wash to the west and the town of Sheringham to the east, and there is seldom a day in the year when some rarity is not in the vicinity.

The winter season brings big flocks of both geese and waders, especially in the western corner, near to the village of Snettisham. On a high tide a substantial number of the waders using the intertidal mudflats of The Wash move to the small complex of gravel pits and islands here for roosting and, on a particularly high tide in season, up to 50,000 Red Knots, 11,000 Dunlins and 6,000 Eurasian Oystercatchers may be using this tiny area at the same time. The sight and sound of them packing on to the islands and spits and flying about is incredible and, indeed, even on a modest tide the Red Knots still make an impressive spectacle on the flats themselves. These birds are famed for their gigantic gatherings, the flock moving as one amorphous mass, its edges moving back and forth like plumes of smoke.

Remarkably, that is not the only splendour of Snettisham. At dawn and dusk between October and February, a large flight of Pink-footed Geese also passes over the reserve as the birds commute from their roosting grounds on the salt marsh to the inland fields, where they graze on grain or potatoes. Indeed, this spectacle is

Above: Barn Owls can be difficult to see in parts of Britain, but in Norfolk they are common and conspicuous at many of the key birding sites.

repeated right along the coast as far as Holkham, some 30km to the east. The geese fly high and their V-formations make handwriting in the skies, often to a backdrop of the rising or setting sun, while the merry *ang-ang*, *wick-wick* calls ring down on to spellbound birders. It is estimated that, at the very least, 100,000 Pink-footed Geese from Iceland winter in north-west Norfolk, along with nearly 10,000 Brent Geese from Russia, of the dark-bellied form *bernicla*.

Another of the attractions in north Norfolk is the presence of several scarce passerines that choose these wild, windswept coasts as regular wintering grounds. These include two species that breed primarily in the high Arctic – Snow and Lapland Buntings – plus two birds that are mainly northern montane breeders in Europe – Twite and Shore Lark. All these species scour the dunes and salt marshes for seeds and they can often be found together in flocks. The Snow Buntings are a particular favourite, as they can often be seen in appreciable numbers (200 or more) and their flocks have the endearing habit of 'rolling' forwards, with birds at the back intermittently overflying the leaders to get in front.

The breeding birds of north Norfolk are almost as impressive as the winter visitors and include several scarce species. The farmlands are the English stronghold of the fast-declining Grey Partridge, while other birds that are also being lost from the rural British scene are also present, including Barn Owl, Corn Bunting and Eurasian Tree Sparrow. Also important are the reed swamp birds, with Bearded Tit, Eurasian Bittern and Western Marsh Harrier all being widespread, if not common. Pied Avocets, close to the northern edge of their range, breed on some of the lagoons within nature reserves – some of which have been specially constructed for the purpose. Terns also occur, especially on offshore Scolt Head Island and on Blakeney Point; Sandwich Terns can number nearly 4,000 pairs altogether.

For many an experienced birder, however, it is really the migration season that gives Norfolk its almost magnetic attraction. Norfolk is one of the closest parts of the United Kingdom to the European continent, and it only takes some kind of easterly blow, with a touch of drizzle, to dump drift migrants unexpectedly on to these coasts. On a good autumn day the many bushes and trees may be alive with migrants, especially Willow and Garden Warblers, Common Redstart and European Pied Flycatcher, and a thorough searching will sometimes reveal a rarity such as Eurasian Wryneck, Red-breasted Flycatcher or Barred Warbler. As the season progresses, Yellow-browed Warblers in October and then Pallas's Leaf Warblers in November brighten the scene. Spring is also very good, with many of the same species as in early autumn, seen in their breeding finery. If conditions are right

Below: A flock of Snow Buntings. These birds occur on the sandy beaches and dunes in winter.

there might be a Bluethroat from the east or a Red-rumped Swallow or European Serin from the south.

Good numbers of waders are present throughout the year in the many pools and lagoons, and on a good day in September it is possible to see well over 20 species, including Curlew Sandpiper and both Little and Temminck's Stints. The many hides on nature reserves such as Cley and Titchwell can allow exceptional views of such birds at close quarters.

The sea-watching scene is just as lively as the comings and goings on land. North Norfolk is excellent for wintering seaduck such as Common and Velvet Scoter, Long-tailed Duck and Common Eider, while other inshore species include Red-throated Diver and Slavonian and Red-necked Grebes. Meanwhile, strong onshore winds in autumn bring skuas in good numbers, together with a few Manx and Sooty Shearwaters. Later on in the year a northerly blow can deliver good numbers of Little Auks from the Arctic.

Not surprisingly, the rarity list is long and includes some jaw-dropping encounters, some of which have gone down in the birding folklore that surrounds this place. For example, one spring both a Laughing Gull and a Franklin's Gull turned up on the very same day, more or less standing next to each other, while many British firsts, including a bewilderingly unlikely Rock Sparrow, have graced this coastline. This is the modern centre of British birding and its status is fully deserved.

CD tracks

TRACK 43: Pink-footed Goose
TRACK 44: Eurasian Wigeon

141

Opposite: North Norfolk is a superb place for geese, including these Dark-bellied Brent Geese, 10,000 of which visit in winter after a long flight from their Russian breeding grounds.

Below: A typical winter scene on the north Norfolk coast: masses of birds to keep the birders happy.

The Outer Hebrides

Britain is something of an enigma in terms of its birding heritage. On the one hand, birding is perhaps more popular here than just about anywhere else and the flagship conservation organization, the Royal Society for the Protection of Birds, is one of the best, if not the best, in the entire world. On the other hand, the actual birdlife of the islands is surprisingly modest. Of the 560 or so species that have been recorded up to 2010, less than half are breeding or regular wintering species and the rest are made up from a very long list of freak waifs and strays. You might even say that the birding facilities, knowledge and know-how are a lot more impressive than the birds.

However, there are two exceptions to the generally impoverished state of the avifauna. The breeding waders are of international importance and even more so are the seabirds. And nowhere in Britain are these two groups of birds so prevalent, and found in more breathtaking scenery, than in the archipelago of the Outer Hebrides (which is also known as the Western Isles).

The Outer Hebrides lie, on average, about 50km off the north-west coast of Scotland. The main archipelago measures about 200km from north to south, while a great deal of bird interest also lies in a cluster of outlying island groups, such as St Kilda, 64km further out into the wild North Atlantic. On the main island chain there is an intriguing grading of habitats from west to east: the west coast is rimmed with long beaches of shell-sand, often backed by dunes. Just inland of this is a unique habitat known as machair, which is grassland growing on a mixture of shell-sand and peat. The dry areas of machair are farmed in a traditional manner, while the wet areas provide low-lying, rich pools. Further inland still, the land becomes dominated by peat bogs and moorland dotted with lakes, until it reaches the rugged, rocky coast on the eastern side, where every few kilometres the coast indents to form an inland finger of sea, known locally as a sea loch. It is estimated that, taking both saltwater and freshwater bodies into account, there are some 6,000 lakes in the Outer Hebrides. On the whole, the land is low-lying, and the highest point in the whole archipelago is only 799m above sea level.

The peat bogs and machair form superb breeding habitat for waders and the densities of breeding birds here are among the highest in Europe. As a general rule, the northern islands of Lewis and Harris provide the best moorland habitat, with large populations of European Golden Plover, Common Greenshank and Dunlin, while the southern trio of North and South Uist and Benbecula

provide the cream of the machair, with high densities of Common Snipe, Common Redshank and Common Ringed Plover. Every year a few Red-necked Phalaropes, extremely rare breeders this far south, turn up and sometimes they nest successfully.

In such a watery habitat it is perhaps not surprising that wildfowl also feature strongly. The Outer Hebrides maintain an impressive population (300 pairs) of entirely wild Greylag Geese (the rest of the British breeding population consists of feral birds) and there are also significant numbers of Mute Swan, Common Eider and Red-breasted Merganser. The lakes provide good habitat for both Red-throated and Black-throated Divers, making this a perfect place to compare their breeding ecology. Black-throated Divers breed by large lakes that provide fish on site, while Red-throated Divers nest on often minute, sterile pools and they commute back and forth from the sea to deliver fish to their young.

While a few seabirds breed on the cliffs on the north coast of Lewis, the really impressive colonies occur far offshore. Some of these are important nationally and internationally. Sula Sgeir, off the northern tip of the main archipelago, hosts 10,000 pairs of Northern Gannet and is the only place in Britain where young

Top: On the outlying Hebridean island of St Kilda there is an incredible population of a quarter of a million breeding Atlantic Puffins.

Above: The western coasts of the archipelago are low-lying, with beaches of shell-sand and a unique habitat known as *machair*.

Gannets are harvested for food. Each year, the hunters spend two weeks on this remote rock and collect up to 2,000 youngsters. In the last few seasons a misplaced Black-browed Albatross has also graced these inaccessible cliffs. Meanwhile, the fearsomely isolated North Rona, 71km out in the Atlantic, hosts a major population of European Storm-petrels. The Shiant Islands hold a big colony of approximately 76,000 Atlantic Puffins (and also, curiously, Britain's only population of Black Rats), while the Flannan Islands, 32km west of Lewis, provide breeding habitat for both European and Leach's Storm-petrels (several thousand pairs of each).

However, it is St Kilda, 64km off North Uist, that is by far the most famous for its seabirds, and no wonder: half a million pairs of various species breed there. A world heritage site with a rich history, this cluster of four small islands is all that remains of a long-extinct volcano. Looming above the stormy waters of the North Atlantic, where the heavy swell blights the lives of seabird-counters forced to use a boat, St Kilda was bypassed by the erosion of the last Ice Age and stands proud as a towering lump teeming with cliff-dwelling birds. Indeed, the cliffs on the island of Hirta, the largest island, are a sheer drop of 430m, the highest in Britain.

Opposite: The Northern Gannet colony of Sula Sgeir is 'farmed' by the local people for two weeks of the year.

Above: The Common Guillemot crowds together in uncomfortable looking colonies on steep cliffs.

Above: One of the specialities of St Kilda is not a seabird, but the large local race of the Winter Wren.

CD tracks

TRACK 45: Corncrake
TRACK 46: Twite

Remarkably, this remote outpost has a long history of human settlement. People are thought to have made it here 5,000 years ago and to have introduced the islands' unique breed of sheep. These Soay Sheep are still present today and are undergoing intensive genetic study because of their isolation. What is certain is that the islands were occupied for some 2,000 years, until being abandoned finally in the 1930s, leaving their ruins to breeding Common Starlings of the local race and to the unique 'St Kilda Wren', a rare, large, island form of the Winter Wren.

The numbers of seabirds are indicative of the huge importance of the Outer Hebrides. These islands hold the world's largest colony of Northern Gannet (at least 60,000 pairs – a quarter of the entire population), some 90 per cent of Europe's Leach's Storm-petrel (49,000 pairs), about 250,000 pairs of Atlantic Puffin (half of the British population), 62,000 pairs of Northern Fulmar, 22,000 pairs of Common Guillemot and 150 pairs of Great Skua. Many of these numbers are necessarily approximate, because of the extreme difficulty of counting and the high numbers involved.

Another seabird spectacular of the Outer Hebrides is of a quite different kind – an impressive regular return passage of rare, high-Arctic breeding skuas, moving to and from their wintering quarters off the west coast of Africa. The numbers of Long-tailed and Pomarine Skuas may sometimes run into the thousands during the peak spring passage in May, while fewer birds are recorded in the autumn. These movements are very concentrated and, in the case of the Long-tailed Skua, last from 9th to 24th May. The birds tend to pass in small parties, flying at a steady pace over the waves. Theirs is a long journey, from Equatorial waters to Arctic coasts, and in the case of the Long-tailed Skua, the precise location of the wintering areas is not yet fully known.

Yet, exciting though these skuas are, their appearance off the Outer Hebrides is somewhat peripheral. They neither breed here nor spend their off-season – much like most species on the British List, in fact.

Below: Great Skuas patrol seabird colonies, and often ambush parents of other species that are bringing in food for their young, intimidating them into dropping the meal.

148 # Lake Myvatn

SITE RANK | 22

HABITAT | Large, shallow, freshwater lake, river, moor and bog

KEY SPECIES | Barrow's Goldeneye, Harlequin Duck, other ducks, Gyr Falcon, Rock Ptarmigan, Red-necked Phalarope

TIME OF YEAR | Breeding season: late April to August. Avoid the period from June to August because of the swarms of biting insects

Ask any birder about Iceland and one single locality is almost certain to spring into their mind – Lake Myvatn. There can be few countries, especially in Europe, which are so closely associated in the ornithologist's consciousness with one specific place. Yet few single localities are quite as extraordinary as the Myvatn–River Laxá ecosystem, in the north-east of this large, chilly Atlantic island. It is very much the jewel in Iceland's crown.

Lake Myvatn happens to be Iceland's fourth largest lake, with an area of $37km^2$. But what makes it most unusual is that it is almost entirely spring-fed, rather than river-fed. Rains are absorbed quickly into the surrounding bedrock and re-emerge as mineral-rich springs all around the lake, together producing a net inflow of 35 cubic metres of water per second, most of which eventually exits from the west corner as the River Laxá. Fed by the sunlight, algae grow abundantly in these fertile waters and provide food for midges and blackflies. These insects, indeed, are found in such vast abundance here that they have given the lake its name: Myvatn is Icelandic for 'Lake of Flies'.

One of the results of this invertebrate bounty is that this place is an absolute paradise for ducks. More species (15) breed here than anywhere else in Europe and perhaps the world. And whilst the flies provide ample sustenance for the adult wildfowl, they are even more crucial for the young, and their presence is a major contributory factor in making this such a duck nursery. Two other aspects of the wetland are also important: the whole lake is extremely shallow, never more than 4m deep (average 2m), and it is topographically varied, with myriad inlets and islets. The depth allows the ducks to obtain food easily and the topography provides many and varied breeding sites.

As for the ducks themselves, Iceland's position between the European and North American continents means that the cast list is drawn from both sides of the Atlantic, and two primarily New World species, the Harlequin Duck and Barrow's Goldeneye, breed nowhere else in Europe. The Harlequin Duck is widespread on the island but Barrow's Goldeneye is almost confined to the Myvatn area, with 90 per cent of its population found here. In North America this duck nests in holes in trees, but here in Iceland it would quickly become extinct if it had to depend on these, since no large trees grow here at all. Instead it utilizes holes of a different kind. The whole Myvatn area is highly active volcanically (there are hot springs near the lake) and females often fly out from the lake in groups to the lava fields to look for a suitable crater or burrow in which to nest, a habit unique to this

Left: Fish-eating Slavonian Grebes are common breeding birds on Iceland's premier birding lake.

Above: Despite its size (37 square kilometres), Lake Myvatn is entirely fed by springs.

region. The birds also use holes in buildings, and visiting birders are sometimes met by the incongruous sight of a female Barrow's Goldeneye peering down a rooftop chimney!

The other star species is the Harlequin Duck, a bird of exquisite colour and pattern, which is a specialist in feeding in turbulent waters. These delightful ducks, top of most visitors' 'wanted' list, are easily seen in the River Laxá, which almost certainly has the highest breeding concentration in the world. In summer

the Harlequin Duck specializes in foraging upon blackfly larvae, which tend to be most numerous within these highly oxygenated, fast-flowing waters; when the adult flies emerge in August, they provide food for the young.

The population of Harlequin Duck in this area is about 250 pairs, while Barrow's Goldeneye now numbers about the same, having been in sharp decline in recent years. After breeding, the Harlequins leave the area and indulge their passion for turbulent water along the coasts. Barrow's Goldeneyes, meanwhile, mainly sit out the winter at Myvatn in patches of unfrozen water.

Aside from these specialities, the most numerous duck at Myvatn is the humble Tufted Duck, a rather common European species. In 1970 this diving duck, which feeds on freshwater molluscs as well as the ubiquitous midge larvae, overtook the Greater Scaup in abundance at Myvatn and now outstrips it four to one (6,000:1,500 males). The scaup takes fewer snails than the Tufted Duck and more crustaceans. These species are closely related, and when the females lead their broods on to the lake (late July onwards), the ducklings sometimes become intermixed.

Opposite: A Rock Ptarmigan in spring plumage. This gamebird is common on the surrounding moorland and is a major prey item of the Gyr Falcon.

Below: The stunning Harlequin Duck is confined in Europe to Iceland. At Myvatn it is usually seen on the turbulent waters of the out-flowing River Laxá.

Above: The presence of Great Northern Divers in summer is one Iceland's several links to the avifauna of North America. The others are the Harlequin Duck and the Barrow's Goldeneye.

CD tracks

TRACK 47: Common Scoter
TRACK 48: Snow Bunting

Myvatn attracts a number of other ducks to its water. Among the diving ducks the most interesting are the Common Scoters (approximately 350 males), which are rare elsewhere in Iceland; for food, they favour crustaceans over midge larvae. Long-tailed Ducks (150 males) have similar tastes. The Red-breasted Merganser (700 males) and Goosander (15 males), on the other hand, are both specialist fish catchers. One other diving duck, the Common Pochard, used to breed in very small numbers but has done so only sporadically since the 1950s. Among the surface-feeding ducks the most numerous is the Eurasian Wigeon, with about 1,000 pairs, followed by the Gadwall (nearly 300), the Mallard (about 200), the Eurasian Teal (50–100) and the Northern Pintail (20–40). Northern Shovelers are sometimes seen in spring and may breed regularly in very small numbers. All the dabbling ducks feed on the midges.

Not surprisingly, the lake quite frequently attracts rarer wildfowl. The most regular of these is the American Wigeon, which makes a habit of appearing during the summer, and up to three have been present at the same time. Another possibility is the Ring-necked Duck, while Steller's Eider and Ruddy Duck have also been recorded – the latter a good candidate for a genuinely wild vagrant.

In addition to the ducks, Lake Myvatn offers an excellent supporting cast of other birds. One of these, the Great Northern Diver, is another of the New World brigade; along with Barrow's Goldeneye and Harlequin Duck it has its European headquarters in Iceland and a few pairs nest in the district. The Slavonian Grebe is common (about 600 pairs) and hard to miss, and the gloriously plumaged Red-necked Phalarope can be seen almost everywhere, spinning in the water as it picks midges from the surface. These waders are as sociable as they are approachable.

If you can tear yourself away from the lake for a while to visit the lava flows and moors, you are certain to stumble across the Rock Ptarmigan, which is common here. That is exactly what the Gyr Falcon is intending to do. This large and spectacular raptor is a major predator of ptarmigan in Iceland; indeed, it is thought that predation is such that the ptarmigans have a slightly different breeding system here than they do elsewhere. Instead of being monogamous, the birds seem to have no more than casual relationships; life, it seems, is too short for serious commitment. Other species found hereabouts include the ubiquitous Snow Bunting, Redwing and the Icelandic race of the Winter Wren.

But it's the ducks that will live long in the memory of the visitor.

Below: The Gyr Falcon is a major predator of the area, taking a wide range of birds and other prey.

154 # Falsterbo

INFORMATION

SITE RANK | 6

HABITAT | Coast, heath, marshes, woods and gardens

KEY SPECIES | Big numbers of raptors (including European Honey-buzzard, Red Kite, Rough-legged Buzzard and rarities), finches, tits, waders, pigeons, wildfowl, Black Woodpecker, Spotted Nutcracker

TIME OF YEAR | A migration site, best in autumn, from late August to the end of October

Falsterbo, in southern Sweden, is one of the greatest migration watch points in the world. Its fame, though, doesn't just stem from the vast stream of migrants of all kinds that pass through in the autumn, which may total 100,000 birds in a single day, nor even from the astonishing 356 species that have been recorded in an area of not much more than 50km^2. Falsterbo's fame also derives from the long-term scientific studies that have been conducted here, which have helped to uncover many secrets about birds' abilities to orientate themselves during migration. There has been a bird observatory here since 1955, making it one of the oldest in existence, and it is probable that no other set-up in the world has contributed so much to our understanding of this wondrous phenomenon.

Bearing in mind that Falsterbo is an unremarkable mixture of cultivation, woodland and heath on the low-lying mainland of southern Sweden, one might ask what is so special about it? The answer is a quirk of geography. Falsterbo, you might say, is a peninsula at the end of a very big peninsula. Any birds migrating south from the Swedish hinterland are funnelled naturally by their dislike of long sea crossings into the ever-decreasing tip of the right arm of southern Scandinavia. At the very south-western extremity of this tip, facing the Danish island of Sjaelland only 20km away, lies the small peninsula of Falsterbo, jutting almost apologetically into the Baltic Sea. It's the last crossing before the European mainland for a high proportion of the estimated 500 million birds that pass through southern Scandinavia each autumn, on their way to their wintering grounds in the milder parts of Western Europe and beyond. Between late August and the end of October, untold millions of birds take off from this small spit of land and leave the Scandinavian mainland behind.

Although the overall variety of bird species is superb, what has really made Falsterbo's reputation is the numbers of raptors that pass through here. Almost 30 species have been recorded altogether, which is impressive enough, but it is the sheer potential numbers that coax visiting birders to come here from all over Europe to witness the spectacle. Up to 14,000 individual raptors have been counted passing over in a single day. Daily totals of certain species, such as Eurasian Sparrowhawk, routinely exceed 1,000, with similar totals for Common Buzzard and slightly fewer (600) for European Honey-buzzard. Needless to say, these birds make a spectacular sight, especially in mid-morning during light south-westerly winds, when the air seems to be full of shapes soaring to gain height before they break out over the sea. Many of these fleeting visitors also live

Left: The well worn paths around Falsterbo have been worked by generations of birders.

Above: Falsterbo is one of Europe's finest migration watchpoints, especially in autumn. Bohemian Waxwings are among the many attractions.

Above: More than 10,000 Common Buzzards pass over the peninsula in an average autumn.

up to their predatory nature by attacking smaller birds en route, especially Eurasian Sparrowhawks and Merlins, which frequently follow travelling flocks of small passerines over the water.

The seasonal numbers of raptors illustrate the importance of Falsterbo most effectively. In the course of the whole autumn the average total counts for the commoner species are as follows: Eurasian Sparrowhawk 15,300, Common Buzzard 10,500, European Honey-buzzard 5,000, Rough-legged Buzzard 1,100, Western Marsh Harrier 680, Red Kite 630, Common Kestrel 400, Osprey 240, Hen Harrier 210 and Merlin 200. Other regular migrants that pass through in smaller numbers include White-tailed and Golden Eagles, Montagu's Harrier, Eurasian Hobby and Peregrine Falcon. Not surprisingly, rarities often get mixed up with all these birds. Both Greater and Lesser Spotted Eagles are recorded from time to time, and in recent years increasing numbers of Pallid Harriers have also been turning up.

As you might expect, each species has its own peak time of appearance. Western Marsh Harrier and European Honey-buzzard are commonest from late August to early September, while Red Kites peak in the third week of September and both Common and Rough-legged Buzzards hit their greatest passage in mid-October. On the whole, go for variety in mid-September and for big numbers in October.

Falsterbo is far from being just a raptor site and, indeed, numbers of other species can be just as impressive. This corner of Scandinavia is arguably the best site in the whole of Europe for seeing the visible movement of smaller day-flying migrants. These include Common Starling, finches, pipits and pigeons. In contrast to such birds as warblers or flycatchers, these migrants begin their daily journeys at dawn, rather than at dusk, and their movements often continue until mid-morning. Daylight, of course, makes it possible for birdwatchers to witness them in action and at times, at Falsterbo, flocks of birds can seem to simply deluge through. If the wind is south-westerly it is perfectly possible to see about 1,000 birds passing by every minute! In such conditions it is easy to be overwhelmed and lose concentration.

From September onwards, each dawn sees crowds of birdwatchers huddled at the very tip of Falsterbo itself, at Nabben. From here flocks of birds stream past

Below: Understandably the birding masses gather at Falsterbo each autumn to watch thousands of common migrants and a sprinkling of rarities.

Below: **Below:** Bramblings are among the commonest of all migrants to pass Falsterbo, often forming mixed flocks with Chaffinches.

from first light, often barely over head height, challenging the birders present to identify them from a few calls. Most of these shapes will be finches, of which the most numerous are Common Chaffinch and Brambling. These closely related birds often flock together and, because of the somewhat subtle differences between them in flight, it is impossible to count them separately. Instead the term 'chaffling' has arisen here, for convenience. On a good migration day 10,000 'chafflings' may pass Falsterbo and, exceptionally, 500,000 have been seen in a 12-hour period. Flocks of these birds are a common sight from late September to the middle of October.

Many other species pass by as well, of course. The average seasonal totals for the more numerous visible migrants include 207,000 Common Woodpigeons, 134,000 Common Starlings, 40,000 Western Yellow Wagtails, 32,000 Western Jackdaws, 30,000 European Greenfinches, 26,000 Common Linnets, 24,000 Eurasian Siskins, 23,000 Barn Swallows and 20,000 Tree Pipits. The seasonal total of 17,000 Blue Tits will also surprise the many European birders who are unaware of how migratory this species can be. These small birds often seem to baulk at the shore at first, making several false starts before finally committing themselves to crossing the sea.

As with the birds of prey, a whole host of less common species and rarities can also become caught up in these movements. Notable regulars include the Spotted Nutcracker, Bohemian Waxwing, Red-throated Pipit and Lapland Bunting. Even Black Woodpeckers are regularly seen in the lighthouse garden, although they are not resident and both their origin and destination are obscure.

Nevertheless, steps are continually taken at Falsterbo to try to understand the patterns of migration of the visitors. The first scientific studies and censuses were carried out here in the 1940s and ringing has taken place ever since the 1950s. Since 1980, standardized trapping in the lighthouse garden has given insights into how bird populations are faring. In conjunction with the University of Malmö, much pioneering work has been undertaken at Falsterbo into the biology of migration as a whole.

For birders, though, the science is an afterthought. For a few months in autumn, the entrancing and thrilling spectacle of mass migration in this small part of Sweden is all that counts.

Above: Despite its importance to thousands of small birds, Falsterbo will probably always be most famous for its flights of raptors. European Honey-buzzards are seen from late August to early September.

CD tracks

TRACK 49: Spotted Nutcracker
TRACK 50: Brambling

Matsalu Bay

INFORMATION

SITE RANK | 19

HABITAT | Shallow sea, reed swamp, meadow, islets, woodland

KEY SPECIES | Barnacle and Lesser White-fronted Geese, Long-tailed Duck, Common Crane, Eurasian Bittern, Steller's Eider

TIME OF YEAR | A key migration site, best in May; slightly less productive in autumn but still good. Excellent for breeding birds but quiet in mid-winter

Matsalu Bay is one of the most important wetland areas for birds in the whole of Europe. This is not so much because of its breeding habitats, although these are very rich; neither is the site famous for the birds that spend the winter here. Instead Matsalu is most celebrated as a staging site for migratory birds, equivalent, if you like, to a roadside service station. Birds turn up, stay for a short while to refuel, and then move on. Matsalu has a prime position on the East Atlantic Flyway, the major route between birds' wintering grounds in Western Europe or Africa and the vastness of the Arctic tundra, and therefore the travellers can pass by in staggering numbers. It is estimated that at least one million waterbirds traverse the area each spring, peaking in the first half of May; about a third as many pass by in autumn, between August and October. On a good day the spectacle of mass migration here can be truly astounding.

This is a place of open landscapes and large flocks. The bay itself is an east–west-facing inlet, 18km long and up to 5km wide, surrounded by coastal fields and, further inland, by reed swamps and floodplain meadows. There are also about 60 low-lying islets, some in the bay and some in the Moonsund area on the coastal side; on the inland fringes of the core reserve are also a few deciduous and mixed woodlands. Such diversity of habitat is an open invitation for a rich avifauna; besides the many migrants, there are about 170 species that breed on the nature reserve itself.

The waters of the actual bay are shallow, nowhere more than 5m deep, providing superb feeding areas for ducks and divers. On a busy day in May the dull-grey waters can be dotted with swimming birds as far as the eye can see, with many more passing by in flying flocks, sometimes overhead. These may include simply thousands of Long-tailed Duck, Common Scoter, Common Goldeneye, Tufted Duck, Common Pochard and Greater Scaup, together with hundreds of Red-throated and Black-throated Divers and smaller numbers of such birds as Goosander and Smew. Sooner or later the less-expected species make an appearance: birds such as Velvet Scoter and, if your luck is in, perhaps a few Steller's Eider, which are something of a feature at Matsalu. Just to add to an already impressive spectacle, many of these wildfowl cannot resist the opportunity, even on migration, to engage in bouts of courtship while resting in the bay, and the waters may seethe with excited activity: Long-tailed Ducks pointing their tails skyward, Common Goldeneyes head-throwing and Tufted Ducks peering. The loud yodelling calls of the numerous Long-tailed Ducks

Left: Shallow waters with fringing vegetation are a potent combination for a rich variety of birds.

Below: In May, Black-throated Divers pass through, sporting their best spring finery.

mix with the plaintive piping of scoters and the suggestive croons of the locally breeding Common Eiders, making the whole experience of sea-watching at Matsalu Bay unforgettable.

Fringing the bay are coastal meadows where geese and swans graze, often as impressively numerous as the ducks. At least 20,000 Barnacle Geese pass through Matsalu Bay every spring, together with a similar combined number of Bewick's and Whooper Swans, about 10,000 Greylag Geese and several thousand Bean and Greater White-fronted Geese. It is well worth searching among these goose flocks for the occasional rarity: Red-breasted Geese have been known to mix in with the Barnacles, and in recent years the nature reserve has become a noted site for the perilously rare Lesser White-fronted Goose. This species can be hard to pick out among the distant flocks of Greater White-fronts but in 2004, for example, an impressive gathering of 20 was present for a few days.

One of the more unusual delights of birding at Matsalu is the system of high viewing platforms set up to enable you to see for great distances over the

Opposite: A summer-plumaged Red-throated Diver. Hundreds of divers may be seen in a single day during spring migration.

Above: A male Greater Scaup comes in to land, one of thousands that may pass Matsalu Bay on migration.

surrounding landscape. One of these (Kloostri) is, quite literally, a watchtower, a relic of the time when Estonia was an outpost of the old Soviet Union; these days it is put to much better use! There are five main towers and they vary in height from 6m (Keemu) to a giddying 21m (Suitsu), the latter overlooking a patch of forest. As an illustration of how good these towers can be, in May 1997 a group of birders recorded 128 species of bird from the 8m-high Haeska tower in a period of just 24 hours.

Several towers have good views over reed swamp, of which there are some 3,000 hectares in the reserve overall. The ecologically fussy Eurasian Bittern breeds in this habitat (the reed beds must be just right), with about 15 booming males, and there are also high numbers of breeding Spotted Crake, Western Marsh Harrier, Great Reed and Savi's Warblers and, in more open areas, Black Tern. Inland from here are the alluvial meadows, rich grassland areas often overgrown with willow; these have significant, but currently declining, populations of waders, which include a few Ruff and the occasional Great Snipe, a globally threatened species. Birds such as Corncrake, Thrush Nightingale, Common Rosefinch and River Warbler also occur here.

Below: Matsalu Bay is a major staging area for geese and swans. These are Whooper Swans on their way north to breed.

Once autumn begins the scene is again set for impressive migratory movements, and one of the most distinctive differences from the spring is the appearance of large numbers of Common Cranes. These arrive from their northern breeding grounds from mid-August, peak in mid-September and have all but disappeared by early October. During their stay, numbers may build up to 20,000, making this the largest autumn gathering of Common Cranes in Europe. Autumn can also be a very good time for geese, and numbers may actually exceed those recorded in spring. Few of the cranes remain here for long; winters are harsh and most of the birds evacuate, leaving Matsalu Bay, for a few months at least, a shadow of its former vibrant self.

Above: Ducks on migration, such as this Common Goldeneye, often cannot resist the urge to indulge in a little courtship display on the water.

CD tracks

TRACK 51: Barnacle Goose
TRACK 52: Long-tailed Duck

166 Kuusamo

INFORMATION

SITE RANK | 27

HABITAT | Taiga, with coniferous woodland, lakes, bogs

KEY SPECIES | Red-flanked Bluetail, Greenish and Arctic Warblers, Rustic and Little Buntings, Siberian Jay, rarities

TIME OF YEAR | Spring and early summer, with June the peak month

Below: The Arctic Warbler is one of several rare breeding species in eastern Finland that migrate to Asia for the winter.

Opposite: Old-growth spruce forest is a prime habitat in the taiga, and is home to many of its best birds.

The northern coniferous forest belt, known as the taiga, is the largest ecosystem in the world, stretching right the way across Eurasia and North America, roughly between latitudes 52°N and 66°N. It is characterized by endless tracts of a small number of coniferous tree species, with the monotony interrupted by a splendid mix of wetland habitats, including bogs, meadows, lakes and marshes. Compared with North America and Siberia, there is very little taiga vegetation left in Europe and it is arguably at its very best only in Finland. And as far as birders are concerned, the richest taiga habitat of all is found near the small Finnish town of Kuusamo, in the east of the country, close to the Russian border. Here it is hillier than in most of the surrounding area, with calcareous soils and a relatively large amount of old-growth, mossy spruce forest, and as a result there live a number of species that are found nowhere else in Europe, except for parts of Russia – and even there they can be very rare, being well to the west of their usual range.

The Kuusamo area is renowned among Finnish birders not just for rarities but also for the sheer variety of birds that can be found here at certain times of the year. That's why the town hosts an annual bird race, where teams from all over Europe come over to outdo each other in counting the number of species they can see or hear in 24 hours. The race is held in the second week of June and the winners frequently score in excess of 130 species – remarkable for the latitude and a pretty good score for anywhere in Europe.

If there is one species that has become synonymous with Kuusamo, it is the Red-flanked Bluetail (also known as Orange-flanked Bush-Robin). One of the species that is characteristic of taiga much further east, it is probably the biggest birding prize hereabouts, with both rarity and looks in its favour. There are usually no more than 10–20 breeding pairs in Finland in a given year (plus many more singing males) and they inhabit old-growth spruce forest on slopes. Old growth refers to forest that has been essentially undisturbed by people, meaning that there are plenty of dead and fallen trees and large accumulations of moss on the branches, and here the Bluetails feed both on the ground, robin-style, and up in the branches of the trees. The gorgeous males, with their grey-blue upperparts, flash of orange on the flanks and bright blue tails, are unusual among their peers (chats such as robins and redstarts) by singing in the topmost branches of trees. However, they only sing their clear, melancholy tune sparingly, typically very early in the morning.

For many years the top Red-flanked Bluetail site has been Valtavaara Nature Reserve, to the north of Kuusamo, where the birds first bred in 1969. At the foot of the hill is a lay-by on the road between Valtavaara and Konttainen, where birders typically meet up early in the morning during June to listen for Bluetails and to exchange news. There is a feeding station here that sometimes attracts such sought-after species as Siberian Jay and Eurasian Three-toed Woodpecker, an excellent supporting cast to the extreme rarities.

Just as good for Red-flanked Bluetails is Iivaara, 35km to the south-east of Kuusamo. The habitat is similar, with a trail winding its way up a 470m slope covered by mossy spruce forest. It's also an excellent place for another of the area's specialities, the Rustic Bunting, which occurs in the boggy sections with stunted, moss-covered pines. The Rustic Bunting is another species that, for unknown reasons, has expanded its range further west to colonize the non-Russian parts of Europe, although it has been around for a good deal longer than

Below: The Northern Hawk Owl bucks the trend for its family by hunting almost entirely by day.

Above: One of the specialities of the area, the Rustic Bunting was first recorded as a breeding bird in Finland in the 19th century.

the Bluetail, since at least the 19th century. Its song, sounding like a rich version of a Dunnock, is only heard for a short period at the start of each brood, in May and then again in June, making this species as tricky to pin down as its more illustrious neighbour.

Finland is good bunting country, with another rarity, the Little Bunting, occurring in scrubbier areas than the Rustic, with fewer trees. Both species can be found in the 27,000ha Oulanka National Park, 60km to the north of Kuusamo, while a good current stake-out for Little Bunting is Torankijärvi, where several pairs nest in the willows beside the lake. This species is yet another recent colonist, having first been recorded in 1953.

The taiga forest zone also holds good populations of warblers. Indeed, Finland's commonest breeding bird is the Willow Warbler, and these birds are simply everywhere. However, while no visiting birder will pay this bird anything but scant

attention, they will be earnestly looking for two of its close relatives, the Arctic Warbler and the Greenish Warbler. Both occur in areas with some deciduous trees, the Greenish in mixed forest and the Arctic usually in birch stands, and both prefer lush areas close to rivers. Neither is easy to find. The Arctic Warbler is a treetop bird that has a surprisingly sluggish feeding style compared to its turbo-charged, hyperactive colleague. Numbers of both species vary annually, and in the Greenish Warbler it has been shown that peak numbers coincide with high temperatures and warm south-easterly winds in mid- to late May.

The specialities mentioned up to now are, apart from the Arctic Warbler, all recent, or comparatively recent, colonizers of this part of Europe: the Greenish Warbler in 1937. All five also share a migratory quirk of some significance – none winters in Africa but instead all go south-east to winter in Asia. This can lead to some extraordinary journeys. The Rustic Bunting, for example, flies east for 3,000km or more, hugging the forest and avoiding the steppes of Central Asia, before finally striking out southwards and wintering in South-east Asia. The Arctic Warbler winters in Thailand, Burma and Indonesia, with some individuals travelling up to 15,000km in all. Truly, this curious corner of Finland is a little bit of the Far East among the European taiga.

Whether or not you are seeking rarities such as these, it should be admitted that birding in the taiga is never easy – unless you are looking for Willow Warblers! Most species, as mentioned above, occur at very low densities, and it is perfectly possible to hike for a day or more and only catch up with a handful of sightings. In these wilderness areas the birds can probably see the birders easily enough; indeed Siberian Jays, for instance, have a habit of apparently materializing from nowhere. Visitors who might not have seen these attractive brown and orange species while walking all day might suddenly find that, as soon as they begin to light a fire, the birds find them, having learnt that human fires are associated with food. These birds are omnivores that live in small groups based on an extended family.

However hard the birding is, though, the rewards are undoubtedly high for those persistent enough to reap them. Other exciting species found hereabouts include the Pine Grosbeak, a bird that develops pouches to the side of its palate in the breeding season in order to help it carry more food to the young, and the Siberian Tit, another bird often found in small parties, perhaps best sought out at feeding stations to save the trouble of finding a 'real' wild one. Both Parrot and Two-barred Crossbills join the Common Crossbill in the conifer woods, while other good birds include Hazelhen, Capercaillie and an impressive range of owls, including Pygmy, Tengmalm's and Great Grey – although these are more easily found at nearby Oulu (see page 172).

CD tracks

TRACK 53: Red-flanked Bluetail
TRACK 54: Rustic Bunting

Opposite: The incomparable Red-flanked Bluetail is one of the main attractions for most birders visiting Kuusamo.

Oulu

When birders flick through their field guides and contemplate what birds they have seen, one family in particular is likely to have more gaps than usual – the owls. Few birds in Europe are more difficult to catch up with, owing to various factors: their nocturnal habits, generally retiring character and, especially among those found in the northern forests, their thinly spread and volatile populations. What every birder needs is something of an owl capital, a place where he or she can catch up with many of the species en masse.

It so happens that such a place actually exists: Oulu, the largest city in northern Finland. There is nothing particularly special about the coniferous forests around here; they are exactly what you would expect to find at 65°N. What does make them unusual is their resident network of spies.

In most European taiga forests the owls and other birds are thinly dispersed over a wide area and can be almost impossible to find. However, since Oulu is a population centre and birding is a popular hobby in Finland, even the most elusive species tend to be tracked down by local enthusiasts year after year. Thus it is possible for a visiting birder to tap into this information by hiring a guide and thereby see a wide range of desirable species with minimal effort. It may not be

Right: The Limiganlahti Nature Reserve near Oulu has an excellent range of water birds, including the Terek Sandpiper.

everyone's idea of 'proper' birding but those who have feasted their eyes on some of Europe's trickiest birds tend not to complain too loudly.

Oulu's superb collection of owls is such that, in the spring, it is possible to find eight species within about half an hour's drive of the city, and occasionally the whole set has been seen in a single night. Nowhere else in Europe offers such diversity of these magical birds nor such convenience in finding them. Many of the nests are discovered in April and May, and by the time most birders arrive the adults are feeding youngsters, making for a great show.

The most famous owl at Oulu is the Great Grey Owl, a huge, mottled, smoky-grey bird with yellow eyes and narrow concentric 'growth rings' on the facial disc; the Oulu area may be the best place in the world to see it. Although it looks large

Above: In the breeding season up to eight species of owls may be found within half an hour's drive of Oulu. The Eurasian Eagle Owl isn't the easiest to see, but sometimes it perches on street lights in the city.

enough to carry a birdwatcher away, this bird is actually quite light underneath its thick plumage, and it specializes, as do so many of the northern owls, on voles. These creatures often make burrows under the snow, but such is the Great Grey's hearing that it can detect movements under the white blanket and smash through the crust with its talons. These birds tend to nest in the structures abandoned by buzzards and other birds of prey.

The shy and secretive Ural Owl is another highlight. With its comparatively small, dark eyes and gentle expression, it looks placid, but that totally belies its fearsome nature. Woe betide any birders who approach too close to an occupied nest; they could be viciously attacked, and a few have been badly injured. Thus any encounter with this big bird carries a frisson of danger, something we birders are not really used to; several nests are staked out each year.

Opposite: The Great Grey Owl is usually top of a birder's wanted list. Despite its size, it feeds primarily on small mammals such as voles.

Above: Ecotourism is well developed in these parts.

A Eurasian Pygmy Owl certainly couldn't do you much damage, as this pint-sized predator lives up to its name, being no larger than a Common Starling. It is, nevertheless, a ruthless predator, capable of tackling prey species larger than itself, which, unlike most of the other owls in the area, include a substantial proportion of birds. This is one forest owl that a visitor to Oulu might run into without a guide, since it is common and will often perch high on top of a conifer, even in broad daylight, and call. A much trickier customer is the Tengmalm's Owl, which occupies the same forests. This species is strictly nocturnal, even during the short nights up here, and is often found in the darkest, densest forest interior. This richly patterned species often stares out from its nest hole when people visit a stake-out, glaring with wide-open yellow eyes that produce a slightly mad expression.

Not all the owls around Oulu are strict forest-dwellers. One of the commonest species, the Short-eared Owl, breeds in open areas and bogs, and nests on the ground. The Eurasian Eagle Owl, meanwhile, can be found in the insalubrious surroundings of the city dump and also has a habit of perching on highway street lights. Whereas the Short-eared Owl is numerous, to see the Eurasian Eagle Owl requires being in the right place at the right time.

While all the above species can be found around Oulu every year, two other species are less reliable: the Long-eared Owl and the Northern Hawk Owl. Both are most numerous in good vole years (as indeed are many of the owl and other raptor species); 2010 is the most recent of these. And while the former is a pretty numerous species throughout most of Europe, the latter is highly sought after; however, as often as not birders need to travel 200km north-east to the Kuusamo area (see page xx) to catch up with it. The Northern Hawk Owl is unusual for being entirely diurnal and actually roosts at night. In common with the pygmy owl it often perches on the tops of tall trees, but while the Pygmy Owl has a varied diet, the Hawk Owl is almost entirely dependent on voles during the breeding season.

Between owls, there are plenty of other birds to see. Indeed, Liminganlahti, to the south of Oulu, on the edge of Liminka Bay in the Gulf of Bothnia, is Finland's most important wetland. It was once home to Europe's only population of Yellow-breasted Buntings but the numbers have crashed to nothing recently, perhaps as a consequence of over-hunting on its wintering grounds in southern Asia. Instead, visitors can admire Europe's most westerly population of the singularly odd Terek Sandpiper, as well as such species as Common Rosefinch, Greylag Goose, Black-throated Diver, Spotted Redshank and Western Marsh Harrier. It is also a terrific site for breeding Ruff, with several hundred females breeding. These birds operate a highly unusual 'lek' breeding system, in which males compete among themselves to gain possession of a central territory, to which the females make a

CD tracks

TRACK 55: Eurasian Pygmy Owl
TRACK 55: Tengmalm's Owl

bee-line when they are seeking sperm for their eggs. All male Ruffs look slightly different, even to our eyes – a situation unique in the bird world – and part of the system is that males behave according to the colour code of their plumage. Black- and brown-ruffed males remain on a single lek all season, whereas white-marked birds ('satellites') may commute between leks to obtain the odd opportunistic copulation.

Watching the Ruffs – which display in complete silence – from one of the five observation towers in the Limanganlahti Nature Reserve is certainly a highlight of visiting Oulu. It can almost, but not quite, trump the owl spectacular.

Below: Not all the special birds near Oulu are owls. These are Siberian Jays, which live in the taiga in small family parties.

Varanger Peninsula

INFORMATION

SITE RANK | 18

HABITAT | Arctic tundra, cliffs, coast (mainly ice-free), scrub

KEY SPECIES | Steller's and King Eiders, White-billed Diver, Brünnich's Guillemot, Gyr Falcon

TIME OF YEAR | March to mid-June (peak May to June). Thereafter there are plenty of birds but mosquitoes are a problem

Perched at the northern tip of the European continent, the Varanger Peninsula would be an impressive place even without its birds. The countryside, with its barren, ice-covered rocks, patchwork tundra, colourful scattered houses and towering sea cliffs, has its very own jolting sort of bleakness, and the ever-changing weather, which results from the continuous tussle between the fierceness of the Arctic latitude (400km inside the Arctic Circle) and the mollifying effect of the Gulf Stream, simply serves to provide endless different backdrops for this dramatic landscape. It is a great setting for some fantastic birding.

The area offers the chance to see some northern specialities that are hard to find elsewhere on the European continent. The most famous of them are the eiders, which come here from further east to take advantage of the unusual ice-free winter conditions in the Varangerfjord and around the peninsula (an effect of the Gulf Stream). Three species are easy to find: the Common Eider, a numerous bird of the north European seaboard; the King Eider, a deep-water duck of rough Arctic seas; and Steller's Eider, another Arctic species, which prefers to feed in the shallows. A fourth species, the Spectacled Eider, is a real rarity, having been recorded on just three occasions.

Both King Eider and Steller's Eider use the area as a major non-breeding base. Up to 15,000 Steller's and 5,000 King Eiders arrive in October from their main breeding sites in Russia and can be seen all around the peninsula, the male Steller's, with their glorious butterscotch-brown underparts, black plumes and white head, and the drake Kings with their smart blue-grey heads, red-and-orange bills and bold black-and-white bodies. Both species remain in large flocks well into the spring, and a few, mainly second-year Steller's, remain throughout the summer. A good spot for the summering birds is offshore from the small settlement of Nesseby.

The richly productive waters of the Barents Sea provide the eiders with plentiful molluscs, crustaceans and echinoderms, and they share this bounty with large numbers of Common and Velvet Scoters, Greater Scaup, Common Goldeneye and Long-tailed Duck. The area is also an exceptionally rich fishery, and this attracts a slightly different guild of birds, chief among them the divers. These thick-necked, back-propelled fish-chasers are common in the ice-free waters and, as with the eiders, include in their number a mixture of the routine and rare. Both Black-throated and Red-throated Divers are plentiful and breed, while a small number of non-breeding Great Northern Divers may be seen in the summer. However,

Left: The warming properties of the Gulf Stream ensure that the east-facing Varangerfjord does not freeze in winter.

Below: Up to 15,000 Steller's Eiders may use the unfrozen waters of the fjord in winter, making it by far the best place to see this species anywhere in Europe.

Varanger is most famous for its White-billed Divers. They are primarily winter visitors but, like the eiders, leave a few representatives behind in the summer. On a good day in spring, up to 300 passing birds have been counted from the headland at Hamningberg, on the north-east side of the peninsula, suggesting quite a substantial wintering population.

One of the fish species that spawns off these coasts is the Capelin, a great favourite of another of the region's specialities, the Brünnich's Guillemot. This Arctic auk, which has been known to dive 210m below the surface to find food, breeds on the Varanger Peninsula and just a handful of other places on the European mainland, being found principally in island groups in the Arctic Ocean, such as Svalbard. The Brünnich's Guillemot feeds on the Capelin in the early spring before settling on its breeding ledges by the end of April. A good place to find it is the island of Hornoya, just off the town of Vardo on the eastern extremity of the

Opposite: Some areas inland from the Varangerfjord, especially the Pasvik Valley to the south, hold taiga birds such as the Siberian Tit.

Below: Four species of eider have been recorded in the Varangerfjord, but the exotic Spectacled Eider is a great rarity.

Above: Numerous waders, including the Spotted Redshank, breed in the bogs around the fjord.

CD tracks

TRACK 57: Common Eider
TRACK 58: Temminck's Stint

peninsula. Overall, this is a great location for seabirds, with breeding Common Guillemot, Razorbill, Black Guillemot and Atlantic Puffin keeping the Brünnich's Guillemot company. To complete the set of European auks, the Little Auk also occurs here in winter and may breed occasionally. Other breeding birds include 25,000 pairs of Black-legged Kittiwake, plus European Shag and one of Europe's largest colonies of Herring and Great Black-backed Gulls. White-tailed Eagles, which are numerous at Varanger, and Gyr Falcons, which are scarce, visit these colonies regularly during the summer in search of an easy meal. Arctic, Long-tailed and Pomarine Skuas may also cause their fair share of trouble.

In recent years a colony of Leach's Storm-petrels has also been found on Hornoya. It was probably overlooked in the past because the birds don't enter their breeding colonies until late summer, when most birdwatchers have left the area. This late breeding helps them avoid the attention of predators; in midsummer there is no night-time or twilight to hide the birds, so they delay until there is some darkness at night.

Besides the seabirds, the Varanger Peninsula has many other delights, not least its breeding waders. These include abundant Temminck's Stints, which may perch on top of street lights in the towns; colourful Red-necked Phalaropes, which spin in the pools; Spotted Redshanks, which breed in the bogs; Ruffs; European Golden Plovers; and numerous Purple Sandpipers. The last-named are famous for their remarkable 'rodent run' distraction display, used to lure marauding predators like Arctic Foxes away from their nests, in which they run through the vegetation and squeak like lemmings.

Away from the coast there are several excellent sites for a different suite of Arctic birds. In the south-west of the peninsula are some woodlands, where such species as Arctic and Common Redpolls, Siberian Tit and Siberian Jay occur. The hills and fells in the centre (especially Falkefjell at 548m) are worth checking for Snowy Owl (rare), Long-tailed Skua, Eurasian Dotterel and Bluethroat, while scrubby areas offer such species as Red-throated Pipit. One of the great advantages of this marvellous area is that it is very easy to bird here, with good roads and good accommodation, so all of these different habitats are within comparatively easy reach.

Below: The Purple Sandpiper, famous for its distraction displays, is a common breeding bird of the area.

184 # Svalbard

This might be Europe but not as most of us know it. Situated between the latitudes of 74°N and 80°N and a mere 600km from the North Pole itself at its nearest point, the archipelago of Svalbard is an otherworldly land of glaciers, icebergs, spiky hills (the alternative name Spitzbergen means 'sharp mountains') and fragile, flower-studded tundra. Although adrift 657km north of the North Cape of Norway in the Arctic Ocean and over 1,000km from the nearest airport, this is nevertheless the most accessible truly polar region on earth, with regular flights and tours and a burst of high-summer activity. But with a total permanent human population of around 2,800 in an area the size of the country of Ireland, Svalbard is one place where the presence of humans really does seem incidental. Once you leave the token bustle of the main settlement, Longyearbyen, population 1,500, you find yourself in some of the wildest, loneliest land on earth. The scenery takes your breath away; the wildlife is king. Tread carefully.

It could easily be argued that Svalbard's true marvel lies in its mammal life, with 20 per cent of the world's Polar Bears (3,500 animals; they still outnumber the human residents), plus Walruses, various Arctic-adapted seals, Arctic Foxes and a suite of impressive cetaceans, which includes Narwhal and Beluga. But the birds aren't far behind. Although there aren't many species (less than 50 species breed or have bred), almost all of them are special and some occur in enormous numbers. Several are extremely difficult to see anywhere else.

If one bird stands out, or at least features at the top of every birder's wish list, it is the Ivory Gull. Up to 500 pairs breed on Svalbard, although numbers have been declining since at least 1990, probably because of global warming, and there might only be half this number remaining now. It is the quintessential Arctic bird, a great rarity anywhere south of the Arctic Circle and probably the bird that has reached the farthest north anywhere in the world. The adults fit in well to their habitat, being among the few birds that have completely white plumage, together with a black doe-eye, black legs and a curious green and yellow bill. When settled they have a curious, rolling gait, strikingly similar to that of a pigeon. They have quite powerful flight and are extraordinarily reluctant to swim, preferring to perch on the ice. They have a famously insalubrious diet, which includes carcasses, seal afterbirths and the faeces of Polar Bears. But birders love them.

To see an Ivory Gull is no foregone conclusion, even in Svalbard. The 20 or so colonies are small and scattered, and many are in remote (even for here) places, only reachable on a cruise or special expedition, although some intense birding

Left: The beautiful but scavenging Ivory Gull is Svalbard's main attraction for the birder. Up to 500 pairs may breed.

Below: A typical Svalbard scene. The name Spitzbergen, correctly used for one of the main islands in the archipelago, means 'sharp mountains'.

Below: A rare sight in Europe, a Sabine's Gull in summer plumage. The only breeding pairs in Europe are here, mainly on Moffen Island.

Bottom: Svalbard hosts about one million pairs of plankton-eating Little Auks, but frankly, it's pretty difficult to count them.

from Longyearbyen usually yields a sighting or two. The birds nest in small groups on level tundra, on nunataks or cliffs, often among colonies of the numerous Black-legged Kittiwake. They are usually seen flying around the pack ice in small numbers.

Another much sought-after gull, here found in its only breeding station in Europe, is the Sabine's Gull. This mainly North American species is best known as a pelagic bird, regularly blown offshore to the western coasts of Europe during autumn storms, but here a few pairs nest on the edge of tundra pools, mainly on Moffen Island, in the north-west. Only the most fortunate visitors catch up with another Arctic gull, the rose-tinted Ross's Gull; sadly it is only a rare visitor here.

Another important group of birds on Svalbard are the auks, for which the archipelago is a major stronghold. With rich Arctic seas lapping against undisturbed islands with plenty of cliffs and boulders, the whole area is a paradise for these seabirds, and there are literally millions of them. The most numerous are two high-Arctic specialities, the Brünnich's Guillemot and the Little Auk. The former is a close relative of the Common Guillemot (rare here) but it has a thicker

bill. It dives deeper than its relative and has a more catholic diet, taking squids, crustaceans, worms and molluscs in quantity, as well as fish. There is a colony of 100,000 pairs on Alkefjellet and the population in Svalbard is close to a million. The Little Auk, meanwhile, is even more numerous, with between 1 and 3 million pairs. The birds are almost impossible to count as they nest inside crevices on boulder-strewn slopes, rather than on cliff ledges, but you get an idea of their multitudes as they mill around the colony and especially when a 'dread' occurs. At the approach of a predator, usually a Glaucous Gull, large numbers fly out together from the breeding sites and head out to sea in a swarm, only to return a few minutes later when the peril has passed. They are unusual in feeding their young on plankton, which they gather from around the pack ice and store in a pouch in the throat. Parents may carry as many as 600 small copepods in the pouch at once.

Although these two are the most numerous auks, there are also 20,000 pairs of Black Guillemot and 10,000 pairs of Atlantic Puffin on Svalbard – both of which

Above: Another very rare European breeding species is the Red Phalarope. Svalbard sustains a healthy population.

188

CD tracks

TRACK 59: Arctic Skua
TRACK 60: Little Auk

would be major populations anywhere else – which demonstrates what a superb place this is for the auk family.

The remaining seabirds on Svalbard are an eclectic mix. The Northern Fulmar is the only member of its family to breed, with a healthy population of around a million pairs, almost all of the high-latitude 'blue' form. The only tern is the Arctic Tern (10,000 pairs) and by far the most dominant skua is the Arctic Skua, with up to 2,000 pairs. Great Skuas have only colonized Svalbard in the last 30 years and they have increased to about 350 pairs. The Long-tailed Skua is stymied by the lack of lemmings here (just a handful of pairs hold out) and the Pomarine Skua no longer breeds at all.

There are fewer birds on the land, as one might expect this far north, but naturally they are another fascinating mix. They include waders, ducks, geese and just two 'proper' land birds, which don't like to get their feet wet. One is that astonishing survivor, the Rock Ptarmigan, which incredibly manages to spend the winter in this violent environment by subsisting on fragments of tasteless vegetation; the race here (*Lagopus muta hyperborea*) is confined to Svalbard and Franz Joseph Land, another polar archipelago to the east. The other is the equally indomitable Snow Bunting, the only regular passerine. It is very common and its sweet jingle is a dominant sound of high summer, but all birds evacuate south to mainland Europe in the autumn.

Two waders deserve mention. If you tried to guess which would be the commonest in polar Svalbard, you might struggle to guess that it is the Purple Sandpiper, not best known for its ability to cope in the far north. But the 10,000 pairs here far outstrip every other wader; the rocky conditions clearly suit it. Ten times less common but in second place in population terms is the gorgeous Red Phalarope, here in one of only two stations in Europe (the other is Iceland). In most of its range the Red Phalarope feeds in tundra pools during the breeding season, but here it frequently forages out to sea.

The breeding wildfowl include a goose that thinks it's a seabird. Barnacle Geese usually breed on sea cliffs here, necessitating a perilous jump down for the newly hatched goslings. The other breeding geese are Pink-footed Goose and (Pale-bellied) Brent; the Barnacle and Pink-footed Geese maintain healthy populations in the tens of thousands. The main ducks are Common Eider (27,000 pairs), Long-tailed Duck and King Eider (both about 1,000 pairs).

The geese, along with almost every bird mentioned here, are breeding summer visitors to Svalbard. The Brent Geese migrate to northern Denmark and north-east England; the Barnacle Geese winter in south-west Scotland; and the Pink-feet winter in the Low Countries. The geese are a link between Svalbard and mainland Europe, pulling two very different worlds together.

Opposite: With its remote location, polar climate and deep seas, Svalbard suits the needs of the spectacular King Eider.

Barthel, P.H. and Dougalis, P., *New Holland European Bird Guide*, New Holland Publishers, London, 2008.

van den Berg, A. and Lafontaine, D., *Where to Watch Birds in Holland, Belgium and Northern France*, Hamlyn, London, 1996.

BirdLife International, *Threatened Birds of the World*, Lynx Edicions, Barcelona, 2003.

Chansigaud, V., *The History of Ornithology*, New Holland Publishers, London, 2009.

Couzens, D., *Atlas of Rare Birds*, New Holland Publishers, London, 2010.

Couzens, D., *Collins Birds: a Complete Guide to all British and European Species*, HarperCollins, London, 2005.

Couzens, D., *Top 100 Birding Sites of the World*, New Holland Publishers, London, 2008.

Cramp, S. (ed.), *Handbook of the Birds of Europe, the Middle East and North Africa: the Birds of the Western Palearctic*, Vols 4–6, Oxford University Press, Oxford, 1985–92.

Cramp, S. and Perrins, C.M. (eds), *Handbook of the Birds of Europe, the Middle East and North Africa: the Birds of the Western Palearctic*, Vols 7–9, Oxford University Press, Oxford, 1993–4.

Cramp, S. and Simmons, K.E.L. (eds), *Handbook of the Birds of Europe, the Middle East and North Africa: the Birds of the Western Palearctic*, Vols 1–3, Oxford University Press, Oxford, 1977–83.

Crozier, J., *A Birdwatching Guide to France South of the Loire, including Corsica*, Arlequin Press, Shrewsbury, UK, 2000.

Del Hoyo, J., Elliott, A. and Christie, D.A. (eds), *Handbook of the Birds of the World*, Vols 8–14, Lynx Edicions, Barcelona, 2003–7.

Del Hoyo, J., Elliott, A. and Sargatal, J. (eds), *Handbook of the Birds of the World*, Vols 1–7, Lynx Edicions, Barcelona, 1992–2001.

van Duivendijk, N., *Advanced Bird ID Guide: the Western Palearctic*, New Holland Publishers, London, 2010.

Ferguson-Lees, J. and Christie, D.A., *Raptors of the World*, Helm Identification Guides, Christopher Helm, London, 2001.

Garcia, E. and Paterson, A., *Where to Watch Birds: Southern and Western Spain*, Christopher Helm, London, 2008.

Gill, F. and Wright, M. (IOC), *Birds of the World: Recommended English Names*, Christopher Helm, London, 2006.

Gorman, G., *Birding in Eastern Europe*, WildSounds, Norfolk, UK, 2006.

Hagemeijer, W. and Blair, M.J. (eds) for European Bird Census Council, *The EBCC Atlas of European Breeding Birds*, T & AD Poyser, London, 1997.

Lever, C., *The Naturalized Animals of Britain and Ireland: Mammals, Birds, Reptiles, Amphibians and Fish*, New Holland Publishers, London, 2009.

Marsh, K., *The Good Bird Guide*, Christopher Helm, London, 2005.

Mearns, R. and Mearns, B., *Biographies for Birdwatchers*, Academic Press, London, 1988.

New Holland Concise Bird Guide, New Holland Publishers, London, 2010.

Olsen, K.M. and Larsson, H., *Gulls of Europe, Asia and North America*, Christopher Helm, London, 2002.

Rebane, M. and Garcia, E., *Where to Watch Birds: Northern and Eastern Spain* (2nd edition), Christopher Helm, London, 2008.

Rose, L., *Where to Watch Birds in Spain and Portugal*, Hamlyn, London, 1995.

Snow, D.W. and Perrins, C.M. (eds), *The Birds of the Western Palearctic*, Concise Edition, Vols 1–2, Oxford University Press, Oxford, 1998.

Svensson, L., Grant, P.J., Mullarney, K. and Zetterström, D., *Collins Bird Guide*, HarperCollins, London, 1999 and 2010.

Wheatley, N., *Where to Watch Birds in Europe and Russia*, Christopher Helm, London, 2000.

Full listing of CD tracks